# FIASCO '12

## PLAYSET ANTHOLOGY

### VOL. 3

ISBN 978-0-9883909-8-0

Second Printing July 2016

"When you play, play *hard*."—Theodore Roosevelt

STEVE SEGEDY
EDITING

JASON MORNINGSTAR
ADDITIONAL ARTWORK

JOHN HARPER
COVER DESIGN

NATHAN D. PAOLETTA
LAYOUT

# BOILERPLATE

This Playset Anthology is a supplement to *Fiasco* by Jason Morningstar and is not a complete game.

The playsets in this volume were each originally published as a "Playset of the Month" in 2012.

For more information about *Fiasco* or to download other playsets and materials, visit www.bullypulpitgames.com.

If you'd like to create your own playset or other *Fiasco*-related content, we'd like to help. Write us at info@bullypulpitgames.com.

Special thanks to Matt Fraction and the many authors who wrote these playsets and agreed to let us feature them in this anthology. Their contributions and enthusiasm have helped to make *Fiasco* great!

# TABLE OF CONTENTS

FOREWORD                            6

DE' MEDICI                          8

HAVANA 1953                         22

WHITE HOLE                          32

HOLLYWOOD WIVES                     44

SALEM 1692                          54

HOME INVASION                       64

FLIGHT 1180                         74

HK TPK                              84

HEROES OF PINNACLE CITY             94

BACK TO THE OLD HOUSE               104

TARTAN NOIR                         114

TOURING ROCK BAND 2                 124

WELCOME TO JET CITY                 134

# FOREWORD

Have you ever gone to see a movie, maybe it's the Coen Brothers, maybe it's David Lynch, somewhere in those zones, tonally, and, from the back of the house, during the darker, bloodier, head-caving-innier moments of the film, someone keeps *giggling*[1]?

James Ellroy, in some goddamn dissertation on film noir from somewhere or the other[2]—maybe regarding Losey & Trumbo's THE PROWLER?—reduced the genre's operative theme to an artful two words: *YOU'RE FUCKED*[3]. I know folks that've gone fifty large in debt at various film schools to learn what the Demon Dog of Crime Fiction so brilliantly and reductively revealed there. Noir. You're fucked. I'm fucked, he's fucked, she's fucked. We. Are fucked. Boom! That's noir. Next up: screwball comedy (*YOU'RE RICH AND HORNY*[4].).

I find giggling a wholly reasonable reaction to the soul-leveling revelation of *YOU'RE FUCKED*. I don't know if that's nihilistic glee or gallows humor or some comorbid combination of cognitive catastrophe that yanks guffaws from all that abyss-gazing but it serves me well. It at least keeps me from screaming and weeping most times. Your mileage may vary of course but fuck your mileage, I'm writing this, not you, and when you write your introduction to a FIASCO book you can tell me all about alternative strategies for confronting inescapable doom beyond giggling and I'll read it and take notes accordingly.

*YOU'RE FUCKED* means more than just a *bad day*, or a *bad thing*, a *bad person*, a *bad event*. *YOU'RE FUCKED* means no exit. *YOU'RE FUCKED* means no future. *YOU'RE FUCKED* means there's a Big Black Box with your name on it, and they weld the goddamn door shut behind you once you get tricked inside, because of course you get tricked inside, because without complicity in your own doom you're not *FUCKED* you're just *having a really shitty day*. *YOU'RE FUCKED* means a trap so perfectly constructed the seams vanish, so wonderfully hidden that its activation was but a *fait accompli*, and that the mechanism hides its true intention until it's too late.

Because when *YOU'RE FUCKED* it's always too late.

---

[1] It's me.
[2] Citation needed.
[3] Emphasis his.
[4] Emphasis mine.

I love traps like that. I'm a writer; I love stories like that. I love trying to make the pieces all fit, to machine everything together *just so*. I love trying to create stories where every moment, every sentence, every word drives inevitably to an ending otherwise unimaginable[5]. It's the joy of writing; it's *design*. It's why, I think on some deep weird level, I write at all. Because perfect traps like that don't exist often. Life is complicated and weird and random. The sauce of chaos never comes to a boil no matter how long you sweat and stare at the pot. Nothing makes sense, there is no meaning, God took off and locked the doors behind with all of us trapped inside. All we have are one another, all that matters is the holy truth of the white-hot *NOW* and none of that shit can be controlled or predicted. Life is chaos. We seek meaning. We craft coincidence. We superimpose what we perceive as sanity over events we would otherwise think of as *shitfucking crazy nonsense*. We forever bang on typewriters hoping that typing HAMLET means we are a genius, rather than that, well, sooner or later, it was gonna happen, so why not now?

The joy of FIASCO[6] comes when the line between *game* and *story* blurs and suddenly you're sitting around a table with the brilliant and wonderful souls you allow into your home and you all try to make the perfect Big Black Box. Impose logic, reason, *design*, over the chaotic horror of existence because in story-space, in a game-space, because here we CAN. We aren't just allowed but it's ENCOURAGED. *Draw this map of hell*, we tell ourselves. *Later on we can find our way out.*

It's a nice thought, anyway.

"No character can speak authoritatively from a space which is being continually cut into ribbons of light," wrote Paul Schrader of film noir, and he'd know; he wrote TAXI DRIVER and used to have to sleep with a loaded gun in his mouth. These spaces, dear reader, are dark places positively slashed with light. No one will help you, these stories say; you will not win, this world tells you. Giggling in the dark serves as the only rational response we have to Big Black Box. Fuck you, we're not getting out alive, so why NOT put the *fun* back in funeral?

The thing[7] I love about FIASCO happens when I play and realize *I'm not alone*. There are other warped fuckers like me, sitting in the darkness, giggling too.

Welcome to the Big Black Box of FIASCO. *You're fucked*. Now go have fun.

---

[5] *Trying.*
[6] One of the many joys.
[7] One of the things.

# MATT FRACTION

Writer of *Hawkeye* and *Sex Criminals*

# DE' MEDICI

## THE INNKEEPER'S RECKONING

Florence, 1559: a city of opportunities for men who have the guts to pursue them. Here, struggling artists find rich patrons, visionary architects create their dreams, ruthless mercenaries get lucrative contracts, and shrewd merchants become as powerful as kings.

Ever since the times of Cosimo the elder, the bankers, the Medici, have ruled this city. Sure, way back then it was still called a democracy, but the art, the armies and the votes were all paid with Medici money. The words of the heretic monk Savonarola shook the consciences for a brief time, bringing back a glimpse of the Republic; but the Emperor and the Pope put the Medici back in charge, with Duke Alessandro.

Upon his assassination, twenty-two years ago, the merchants and lords of the city enthusiastically welcomed young Cosimo, the barely 17 years old son of the mercenary warlord Giovanni delle Bande Nere, who had never lived in Florence. The nobles saw him as unexperienced, weak, and an easy puppet to manipulate.

They couldn't have been more wrong.

## MOVIE NIGHT

Nothing Left to Do But Cry (*Non ci resta che piangere*), For Love and Gold (*L'armata Brancaleone*), The Borgias (TV series), Much Ado About Nothing, The Name of the Rose, Prince of Foxes, The Pillars of the Earth (TV series)

## CREDITS

Written by Giulia Barbano and Renato Ramonda

Cover art by Jason Morningstar

Edited by Graham Walmsley and Jason Morningstar

*De' Medici* was Playset of the Month, January 2012.

# DE' MEDICI

A FIASCO
PLAYSET
BY GIULIA
BARBANO
AND RENATO
RAMONDA

# RELATIONSHIPS...

## 1 FAITH

⚀ Brothers in Christ

⚁ Front bench at Sunday's mass in Santa Croce (see notes)

⚂ Penitent and confessor

⚃ Neighbors, devout and not so devout

⚄ Inquisitor and heretic

⚅ We share common beliefs, best kept private

## 2 LOVE

⚀ Spouses in a loveless marriage

⚁ Secretly betrothed

⚂ The shameful mistake of one night

⚃ Tied by a forbidden passion

⚄ Bitter ex-lovers

⚅ Chaste, yet burning for one another

## 3 WAR AND VIOLENCE

⚀ Protector and protected

⚁ Former brothers in arms

⚂ Deadly rivals

⚃ Veterans of a free company

⚄ Hired assassin and target

⚅ Mercenary and employer

# 4 ARTS AND CRAFTS

⚀ Artist and young apprentice

⚁ Artist and patron of the arts

⚂ Rival merchants

⚃ Ex students at Pisa's University

⚄ Skilled laborer (carpenter, sculptor) and supervisor of the Opera del Duomo (see notes)

⚅ Established court artist and young rising star

# 5 AT COURT

⚀ Noble and page/handmaiden

⚁ High ranking parent and bastard child

⚂ Younger cousins in a noble family

⚃ Secret lovers

⚄ Servant and servant's servant

⚅ High ranking noble and lowly subject

# 6 OF LOW MORALS

⚀ Corrupt public officer and rich merchant

⚁ Moneylender and debtor

⚂ Wrongdoers (thugs, housebreakers, pickpockets, thieves)

⚃ Con man and mark

⚄ Members of the same cabal/conspiracy

⚅ Relic peddler and religious zealot

# ...UNDER COSIMO DE' MEDICI

# NEEDS...

DE' MEDICI

## 1 TO GET RICH

⚀ ...through fraud and duplicity

⚁ ...by blackmailing the Archbishop

⚂ ...by robbing a moneychanger

⚃ ...through a once in a lifetime opportunity

⚄ ...by carefully saving every penny over a lifetime

⚅ ...through one huge winning bet at Il Palio

## 2 TO RIGHT A WRONG

⚀ ...by one of the powers that be

⚁ ...to get back at an old love that ended badly

⚂ ...with a public challenge

⚃ ...by one of the faith

⚄ ...to get your name back

⚅ ...to save a life

## 3 TO ABANDON

⚀ ...temptation on the altar of righteousness

⚁ ...the life your family has planned for you

⚂ ...a helpless woman and the child you sired

⚃ ...holy orders

⚄ ...the oath of allegiance to your Lord

⚅ ...the conspiracy

## 4 TO PROVE YOUR REPENTANCE

⚀ …to your loved one

⚁ …from your unforgivable sins

⚂ …to Cosimo himself

⚃ …before you can kill him

⚄ …to a friend you have wronged

⚅ …to an innocent dragged into scandal

## 5 TO DEFEND FLORENCE

⚀ …by silencing a rival

⚁ …by defending Cosimo De' Medici

⚂ …from her own ungodly vanity

⚃ …from Siennese spies, real and imagined

⚄ …with a casual threat of heresy

⚅ …with great enthusiasm but no real effect

## 6 TO COMPLETE YOUR MISSION

⚀ …and write your name in history

⚁ …by returning to your village richer than Croesus

⚂ …by slaying Cosimo

⚃ …by destroying yourself, literally or figuratively

⚄ …whispered in your ear by the Devil

⚅ …by delivering a message of the utmost importance

# …UNDER COSIMO DE' MEDICI

# LOCATIONS...

## 1 IN PIAZZA DELLA SIGNORIA

- ⚀ Palazzo Ducale (*see notes*)
- ⚁ The Loggia dei Lanzi, among the Medici's statues (*see notes*)
- ⚂ The groundworks for the new offices (in Florentine, uffizi) of the thirteen Magistrates of the Arts (*see notes*)
- ⚃ The Tribunale della Mercanzia (*see notes*)
- ⚄ Palazzo Uguccioni (*see notes*)
- ⚅ Arte del Cambio, the corporation of bankers (*see notes*)

## 2 THE NARROW STREETS OF THE CENTER

- ⚀ The filthy streets of the Market after closing hours
- ⚁ Lungarno, in the middle of the night (*see notes*)
- ⚂ The forgotten Roman temple, beneath the potter's shop
- ⚃ The butcher shops on Ponte Vecchio (*see notes*)
- ⚄ The goldsmith's workshop
- ⚅ The Black Boar's Inn

## 3 IN THE COUNTRY

- ⚀ A crossroads on the way to Montalcino (*see notes*)
- ⚁ A monastery in Chianti
- ⚂ A vineyard, precious grapes on the vines
- ⚃ The ancient oak in Balduccio's field
- ⚄ The Old Hangman's Coaching Inn
- ⚅ A hidden bend of the Arno, downriver from the city

# 4 OF THE FAITH

⚀ A hidden alcove in the cathedral, Santa Maria del Fiore (*see notes*)

⚁ The Basilica of Santa Croce, Franciscan convent and seat of the Inquisition (*see notes*)

⚂ A convent of cloistered Carmelite nuns observing the vow of silence

⚃ In the quiet shade of a rich Benedictine cloister

⚄ The confessional in a discreet church

⚅ The two synagogues in the ghetto, a few yards from the Archbishopric

# 5 AT COSIMO'S COURT

⚀ Cosimo's private apartments

⚁ The palace medicinal garden

⚂ Beneath a long oak dining table

⚃ The bedroom of Lucrezia, Cosimo's stunning (and secluded) daughter (*see notes*)

⚄ A secret passage, cleverly disguised

⚅ The busy palace kitchens

# 6 UNSAVORY

⚀ A gambling house

⚁ The back of the undertaker's workshop

⚂ The secret chapel of a small heretic congregation

⚃ Cosimo's informal torture chamber

⚄ A stinking tannery near Ponte Vecchio

⚅ A brothel near the Arno

# ...UNDER COSIMO DE' MEDICI

# OBJECTS...

## 1 RELIGIOUS

- ⚀ Nail from the true Cross
- ⚁ The cathedral's eucharistic chalice, all gold and precious stones
- ⚂ Finely done illuminated bible
- ⚃ The elderly and comatose Benedectine bursar
- ⚄ Cermonial costume of Tlatlauhqui Tezcatlipoca, Aztec God of death and rebirth
- ⚅ Franciscan monk's habit and a hand-drawn map

## 2 UNTOWARD

- ⚀ Forbidden book, put to the Index by the Holy Church (*see notes*)
- ⚁ The ingredients and recipe for the Philosopher's Stone
- ⚂ Lambskin "French letter"
- ⚃ Newborn bastard
- ⚄ Corpse, freshly stolen
- ⚅ Siennese war banner

## 3 OF INTRIGUE

- ⚀ Ring with a secret compartment
- ⚁ Secret dispatch, cyphered
- ⚂ Wooden cross that hides a dagger
- ⚃ Incriminating testimony from a witness
- ⚄ Sleeping draught, prepared a little strong
- ⚅ Overheard secret, that could destroy a reputation

# 4 WEAPONS

- ⚀ Dagger, dripping poison
- ⚁ Butcher's cleaver
- ⚂ Sword, received as heirloom
- ⚃ Clever collapsible bow
- ⚄ Massive block of fine white Carrara marble
- ⚅ Rosary with heavy stone beads

# 5 CURIOUS AND BIZARRE

- ⚀ The stolen plans for one of Leonardo's machines
- ⚁ Two exotic savage beasts, in cages
- ⚂ Ocularia with extremely well crafted lenses from Holland
- ⚃ Siren, mummified
- ⚄ Alchemical oven
- ⚅ The Florentine codex, an Aztec manuscript

# 6 PRECIOUS

- ⚀ Necklace of sapphires
- ⚁ Golden signet ring
- ⚂ Trunk of silver coins, half full
- ⚃ Letter of exchange worth a thousand gold ducats
- ⚄ Perfectly proportioned skull, cut from New World jade
- ⚅ Siennese race-horse named after the Pope

# ...UNDER COSIMO DE' MEDICI

# HISTORICAL NOTES

## SANTA MARIA DEL FIORE

The cathedral, started over two hundred and sixty years ago, was finished in the last century. It's almost ninety years now that the cross was placed over the dome that Brunelleschi designed. Now, it seems that Vasari will be working on the frescoes as soon as he's done with the Uffizi (yes, the biographer of the artists and supreme gossiper, but a fine painter and architect himself). Too bad for the façade, though. It's still the plain stone of old times, and nobody really likes it—but nobody knows how to fix it.

## SANTA CROCE

Santa Croce is the greatest Franciscan church in the world. It holds several chapels, some decorated by Giotto, and it's connected to the Franciscan convent. The refectory, which holds the Crucifix by Cimabue, is undergoing repairs after the 1557 flood. In the last two centuries the Franciscan have held the role of inquisitors in the city.

## OPERA DEL DUOMO

The cathedral of Santa Maria del Fiore has been completed over a century ago, but work isn't over—someone has to maintain the buildings, create new statues and oversee the works. The Opera del Duomo does all that, and gives artists workspace, as it did over fifty years ago with Michelangelo for his David.

## LOGGIA DEI LANZI

A building with wide arches opening on Piazza della Signoria; not more than ten years ago, Cosimo used this lodge to showcase a massive whale caught in the waters of Livorno. He has also commissioned an allegorical statue of Perseus to Cellini, and it now overlooks the piazza, with its bronze serpents reminding the citizen of the pitfalls of the Republic.

# UFFIZI

The thirteen magistrates oversee to the administration of the city, and Cosimo wants them close. He has entrusted Vasari with the design of a new building to hold all the offices of the administration, the tribunal, and the state archives.

# TRIBUNALE DELLA MERCANZIA

The Tribunale della Mercanzia, built two centuries ago, hosts the court responsible to adjudicate controversies between merchants or members of the corporations. Six of the judges are citizen counselors, and six are foreigners, expert at law.

# PALAZZO UGUCCIONI

Home of the powerful Giovanni Uguccioni, a faithful supporter of Cosimo, who personally intervened to make the Palace the most prominent of the Piazza (excluding Palazzo Ducale, of course). The works are almost finished, but it seems like Giovanni will not enjoy the palace, as his health is faltering.

# ARTE DEL CAMBIO

One of the first corporations of Florence, the guild of the bankers and moneychangers was also one of the most powerful and rich. That is, until the Spanish siege, thirty years ago; the Republic confiscated most of their money, and now Cosimo is using the remains to build the Uffizi.

# PALAZZO DUCALE

It used to be called Palazzo della Signoria, from the times when Florence was a Republic, and it hosted the government. Cosimo had it renamed when he moved in with his family, but his wife, Eleonora, fears that life in the busy center is harming her health. She bought a palace on the south bank of the river from the destitute Buonaccorso Pitti, and wants to move the family there.

# HISTORICAL NOTES

DE MEDICI

## THE RIVER ARNO

Lungarno is the name of both the streets on the banks of the river Arno.

Ponte Vecchio is one of the bridges that cross the Arno. For more than a century the butcher's shops have been built directly over it to try and contain the stench.

## LUCREZIA

The fifth daughter of Cosimo, last summer she was given in marriage to Alfonso, prince of Ferrara. Her mother, Eleonora, is keeping her close until she is ready to consumate the wedding—after all, she's barely 14; but now it seems that the father of Alfonso, the duke Ercole, is very ill, and Alfonso might rise to power soon, and reclaim his wife by his side.

## MONTALCINO

Montalcino is the last of the cities under Siennese influence, where the nobles fleeing from cities conquered by Cosimo fled to find refuge.

## THE INDEX

"The Index" of banned books (Cathalogus librorum Haereticorum), has just been issued by the Roman Church. The inquisition is in charge for its application, and it bans whole categories of books (astrology, magic, translated bibles) and the entire works of some authors (including Pietro Aretino, Savonarola, Machiavelli, Erasmus, William of Ockham and Rabelais). Some voices in the Church are already complaining for its harshness, and it might be brought up for discussion during the upcoming sessions of the Council of Trent, which will deal with the Protestants once and for all.

## ALCHEMY

It's well known among the other scholars and practitioners of The Supreme Art that Cosimo has inherited the passion for alchemy from his grandmother, Caterina Sforza. Alchemy was recently banned by the church, though, after being a viable avenue of study and philosophy for the Christian faithful for centuries. Cosimo's pastime is an open secret.

# EXPERIENCIA

## EN MANIPULAR LA

# CARGA

con mayor cuidado y rapidez

Servicio semanal de NEW YORK y NEW ORLEANS a LA HABANA

## GRAN FLOTA BLANCA

**UNITED FRUIT CO.**

# HAVANA 1953

## SUCKERS IN PARADISE

Cuba, 1953. Havana has been called "the sexiest city in the world" and for good reason. The rhythm of the night is fueled by the rhumba beat, cocaine and the dazzling stars of Cuba. The Mob is starting to move in and light up the casinos, flush with easy money and easier dupes.

General Batista's government rules with an iron fist behind the scenes. All the glamour of Miami only 90 miles away and with none of the rules. So why are there armed bands in the hills led by obscure guerrillas like Fidel Castro and Che Guevara?

## MOVIE NIGHT

*Cuban Rebel Girls* (1959), *I Am Cuba* (1964), *Our Man in Havana* (1959), The *Godfather Part II* (1974)

## DRINK RECIPE: CUBA LIBRE

*from the Esquire Drink Book*

# 1/2 ounce fresh lime juice

# 2 ounces white rum

# 2 dashes Angostura bitters

# Coca-Cola

Pour lime juice and rum into a tall glass packed with crushed ice. Add bitters. Fill with Coke. Stir well.

## CREDITS

Written by Chris Bennett

Edited by Steve Segedy and Jason Morningstar

Cover and interior art by Jason Morningstar

*Havana 1953* was Playset of the Month for February 2012.

22

SPIES
MOBSTERS
WHORES
REBELS
PLAYERS
TOURISTS
HAVANA 1953
UN FIASCO ESCENARIO
ESCRITO POR CHRIS BENNETT

# RELATIONSHIPS...

## 1 FAMILY

⚀ Step-siblings

⚁ Ne'er-do-well cousins

⚂ Estranged couple

⚃ Separated at birth

⚄ Father/mother and eldest son

⚅ Aunt/uncle and nephew/niece

## 2 WORK

⚀ Newspaper writer and "source"

⚁ Model and photographer

⚂ Front desk employee and nemesis

⚃ Entertainer and favorite customer

⚄ Doctor and patient

⚅ Musicians

## 3 VISITORS

⚀ "What are we smuggling this time?"

⚁ Tour guide and tourist

⚂ Retirees

⚃ Money burning a hole in their pockets

⚄ Political exiles

⚅ Looking for the "real" Havana

*Habana*

# 4 ROMANCE

⚀ What happens in Havana...

⚁ Unrequited love

⚂ Newlyweds

⚃ Reunited lovers

⚄ Lothario and innocent

⚅ True believers in love

# 5 CRIME

⚀ Pickpocket and fence

⚁ Mob boss and underling

⚂ Criminal on the run and private dick

⚃ Casino cheaters

⚄ Corporate executives

⚅ Loan shark and debtor

# 6 GOVERNMENT

⚀ Diplomats

⚁ Boss and sycophant

⚂ Secret policeman and informant

⚃ Bureaucrats

⚄ CIA case officer and double agent

⚅ Secretarial pool

# ...IN HAVANA

# NEEDS...

## 1 TO GET OUT

⚀ ...of Cuba, forever

⚁ ...of your "prison"

⚂ ...of your obligations

⚃ ...of the Family

⚄ ...from under their thumb

⚅ ...of sight

## 2 TO GET EVEN

⚀ ...with the Batista government

⚁ ...with a business partner

⚂ ...with the Americans

⚃ ...with the secret police

⚄ ...with Meyer Lansky, "the Mob's accountant"

⚅ ...with a rival

## 3 TO GET RICH

⚀ ...through the Mob

⚁ ...by eliminating competition

⚂ ...by any means necessary

⚃ ...by fleecing the rich tourists

⚄ ...by running guns to the guerrillas

⚅ ...from a spin of the roulette wheel

# 4 TO GET RESPECT

⚀ ...from your family

⚁ ...from the citizens of Cuba

⚂ ...from your lover

⚃ ...from Fidel Castro, guerilla leader

⚄ ...from your kids

⚅ ...from the voices inside your head

# 5 TO GET THE TRUTH

⚀ ...about what happened to your brother

⚁ ...about what goes on in that vile place

⚂ ...about General Batista's secret police

⚃ ...about why she left you

⚄ ...about Cuba's past

⚅ ...about the Mob's dirty dealings

# 6 TO GET AHOLD OF

⚀ ...the papers that will prove your innocence

⚁ ...your lover, for just one night

⚂ ...the person who made your father disappear

⚃ ...a rich American

⚄ ...enough drugs to make you forget

⚅ ...the guns that will set Cuba free

# ...IN HAVANA

27

# LOCATIONS...

## 1 HAVANA PROPER

⚀ VIP table next to Frank Sinatra's floorshow at Capri Casino

⚁ Crowded cellar rhumba dance club, off Tin Pan Alley

⚂ Smoke-filled newsroom of the Diario Alerta newspaper

⚃ Feared security room of the Montmartre Casino

⚄ Outdoor stage at the Tropicana

⚅ Masonic building on Carlos III Avenue

## 2 PRADO PROMINADE

⚀ Bridal suite in the Hotel Nacional, wired for sound

⚁ Cafe table attached to a hydraulic lift leading to the basement

⚂ Fausto Theatre at the corner of Prado and Colon

⚃ Switchboard room at the Hotel Sevilla Biltmore

⚄ Sloppy Joe's Bar, innovator of the eponymous sandwich

⚅ Guest car park at the Telegrafo Hotel

## 3 SEASIDE MALECON

⚀ Miramar Yacht Club, attended by waiters in white jackets

⚁ Thatched roof cabana on "La Concha" public beach

⚂ Gentlemen's locker room at the Vedado Tennis Club

⚃ Lobby of Dona Marina's palatial bordello

⚄ Beachside grilled seafood vendor, who sees everything

⚅ Betting windows at the Fronton Jai-Alai courts

## 4 OLD HAVANA

⚀ Hemingway's seat at the Floridita, "Cradle of the Daiquiri"

⚁ Basement of the Columbus Cathedral

⚂ Gran Teatro de la Habana, home of the National Opera

⚃ Stone battlement of the old La Fuerza fortress

⚄ Heavily-guarded Cuban National Bank

⚅ "Misericord" (discipline room) in Santa Clara Convent

## 5 BARRIO COLON

⚀ Aunt Nina club on San Martin St., "attended by pretty girls"

⚁ Flophouse dive with a spy hole into the adjoining room

⚂ CIA safehouse in a seedy apartment building

⚃ Crowded and bloody cockfight in a back-alley

⚄ Casa Marina, luxurious and notorious house of ill-fame

⚅ Bus station at Calle San Lazaro

## 6 OUTSIDE OF HAVANA

⚀ Fidel Castro's guerrilla encampment in the hills

⚁ Leopard cage at the Zoological Park

⚂ Stag film screening room at the Shanghai Theatre

⚃ "Xanadu", palatial DuPont family estate on an isolated beach

⚄ Cheap seats at the Tropic Park baseball stadium

⚅ Abandoned off-shore oil rig owned by Zapata Petroleum


# ...IN HAVANA

# OBJECTS...

## 1 UNTOWARD

⚀ Pictures of high officials *in flagrante* with the local "talent"

⚁ Fashion mannequin stuffed full of high-grade marijuana

⚂ Portable film camera hidden inside a Spanish Bible

⚃ Grainy B&W snuff film involving the Chief of Police

⚄ Black book of cabaret girls' names/numbers with star ratings

⚅ Autopsy photos of "missing" Mafia don

## 2 TRANSPORTATION

⚀ Off-white '52 Pontiac two-door with a body in the trunk

⚁ WW2 German U-Boat, sunk in shallow water

⚂ 1949 Harley-Davidson cop bike, low on gas

⚃ "Pilar" the finest fishing boat in the harbor

⚄ Street merchant's push-cart with a false bottom

⚅ Motorized float, decorated with ostrich feathers for Carnival

## 3 WEAPON

⚀ Hand-crank generator, used for police "conversations"

⚁ Crate of .45 US M3 "grease gun" submachine guns

⚂ Bottle of Veuve-Cliquot champagne, on ice

⚃ German SS combat dagger, with blood groove

⚄ Bacardi rum bottle full of ether

⚅ Russian fully automatic 9mm Stechkin APS pistol

## 4 INFORMATION

- ⚀ Mobster Meyer Lansky's address book, some names scratched out
- ⚁ Map of US nuclear weapon sites in Florida
- ⚂ Payoff list of local officials, with names and prices
- ⚃ Hand-drawn map to a guerrilla arms cache in the mountains
- ⚄ Dictaphone sound recording machine
- ⚅ Cipher book from the Soviet embassy

## 5 VALUABLES

- ⚀ Bag of uncut diamonds in a cold ice chest
- ⚁ Winning numbers for tomorrow's lottery
- ⚂ Handful of $1000 chips from the San Souci casino
- ⚃ Jewel-encrusted box of handmade Partagas cigars
- ⚄ Pair of Havana Tropicana craps dice, always roll 7 or 11
- ⚅ Rolex GMT-Master watch; repair tag says "Che Guevara"

## 6 IDENTIFICATION

- ⚀ Calling card of U.S. stripper "Bubbles" Darlene
- ⚁ Cuban Secret Police ID card for Bernard Barker
- ⚂ Surgeon's medical ID from Nacional Hospital
- ⚃ Cuban visa for "Jack Rubenstein", marked as "informer"
- ⚄ Stolen paybook for Swedish sailor; ship is docked in port
- ⚅ Soviet diplomatic ID, marked "Do Not Question or Hinder"

# ...IN HAVANA

# WHITE HOLE

## "AN OUNCE OF PREVENTION...

...is worth a pound of flesh. So shut your cock-holster and save your own damn life."

The *heroes* aboard Star Station Sigma took one look at that dimensional anomaly and they got the hell out of town.

After the "white hole" (that's what the super-genius science team called it) tore part of the station's hull clean off, the stupid bastards in charge ordered an evacuation. A few minutes after that, they were headed back to Space Legion territory with FTL drives at maximum. But the white hole had busted the lower deck all to hell, damaging many of the escape pods, so a bunch of people got stranded aboard Star Station Sigma. The losers, mostly.

Those left behind: some junior officers with delusions of competence, some hard-drinking pilots who didn't respond to the alarm quickly enough, maintenance staff (glorified janitors), a few asshole security officers, and a bunch of prisoners from the holding area. Now everyone's trying to figure out how the hell we're going to get off this ship. Problem is, the Ax'Tularians hate the Kruk'Chels, the prisoners hate security, and the crew members hate the officers. The station's orbiting a white hole, and everyone's trying to kill everybody else, and we're just a clump of space-waste circling the drain. I should've stuck with smuggling.

## MOVIE NIGHT

*Event Horizon, Alien, Babylon 5, Pitch Black, Deep Space Nine, Pandorum, Sunshine*

## CREDITS

Written by Rafael Chandler

Cover art by Jason Morningstar

Edited by Steve Segedy

*White Hole* was Playset of the Month for March 2012.

# WHITE
# HOLE

A FIASCO PLAYSET BY RAFAEL CHANDLER

# RELATIONSHIPS...

## 1 CREW MEMBERS

⚀ Meek subordinate and abusive superior

⚁ Manipulative schemers

⚂ All-knowing bartender and hard-drinking engineer

⚃ Hotshot rivals

⚄ Frenzied addict and medical officer who supplies the stuff

⚅ Endlessly patient mentor and arrogant protégé

## 2 CRIME

⚀ Murderer and witness

⚁ Space pirate and rival smuggler

⚂ Syndicate boss and cyborg muscle

⚃ "We clean up the mess. No one finds out."

⚄ Honor among thieves

⚅ Innocent convict and accuser

## 3 RELIGION

⚀ Members of the Star cult

⚁ Faithful who hate one another

⚂ Emissaries to the Temple of Ungu

⚃ Agnostic and Unguite proselytizer

⚄ Leader of the Star cult and zealous defender

⚅ Star cult convert and apostate

## 4 FAMILY

⚀ Sibling rivalry

⚁ Married to the same person

⚂ You'd be parent and child if androids had children

⚃ Zero-gravity sex doesn't mean we're married (*does it?*)

⚄ Clones

⚅ Åx'tularian blood bond

## 5 WAR

⚀ War hero and deserter

⚁ Former enemies but enemies no longer

⚂ "Medal or not, I know you were a coward"

⚃ Bound by atrocities

⚄ Fanatic and traitor

⚅ Conscientious objector and prisoner of war

## 6 COMRADES

⚀ Same small town, same backwater planet

⚁ "We discovered the thing together."

⚂ Fast-talking con artist and stoic problem-solver

⚃ Grizzled space veteran and wide-eyed greenhorn

⚄ "You could say we're shore leave buddies."

⚅ Opposite in every way (*every way*) but fast friends

# ...TOO NEAR A WHITE HOLE

# NEEDS...

## 1 TO BE EXONERATED

⚀ ...by finding the proof at last

⚁ ...so that you can go home

⚂ ...in order to get reinstated

⚃ ...even though you're guilty

⚄ ...and forgiven by the only one whose forgiveness matters

⚅ ...by any means necessary

## 2 TO PUNISH THEM

⚀ ...for framing you

⚁ ...even if it was "just an accident"

⚂ ...and make sure she sees it happen

⚃ ...as slowly as possible

⚄ ...and make sure someone else takes the blame

⚅ ...so that the voices stop

## 3 TO GET RICH

⚀ ...regardless of which little people you have to kill

⚁ ...through hard work and honest effort

⚂ ...and send your wealth to the Temple of Ungu

⚃ ...so you can pay the ransom

⚄ ...enough to hire an army of mercenaries

⚅ ...and leave this horrifying galaxy behind

## 4 TO ESCAPE

⚀ …with the one person/clone/android you care about

⚁ …after settling one last score

⚂ …before your treachery is discovered

⚃ …the murderous xenomorph on your trail

⚄ …even if everyone else dies

⚅ …and start all over again

## 5 TO COMMAND

⚀ …your own starship

⚁ …an army of pissed-off clones

⚂ …a squad of very professional androids

⚃ …a pirate ship, filled with plunder

⚄ …Star Station Sigma

⚅ …others to listen to you, just this once

## 6 TO ATONE

⚀ …At the Daluan Citadel on Yemekzi IV

⚁ …even if you won't be forgiven

⚂ …before you plunge into the void

⚃ …for crimes too heinous to name

⚄ …by soaking your hands in their blood

⚅ …even though, whatever, you don't even feel that bad about it

# ...TOO NEAR A WHITE HOLE

# LOCATIONS...

## 1 INTEL-SEC

⚀ B4 Monitoring

⚁ B8 Armory, dripping with xenomorph residue

⚂ C9 Combat holo-training creche

⚃ C17 Records

⚄ B2 Friendly interrogation suite

⚅ B5 Intel-Sec Commander's office

## 2 COMMAND DECK

⚀ A1 Command Center—control helm

⚁ A2 Captain's ready room

⚂ A5 Briefing room

⚃ A1 Command Center—comm station

⚄ A1 Command Center—tactical operations

⚅ A19 Weapons System controls

## 3 LIVING QUARTERS

⚀ C21 Tachyon's Bar and Grille

⚁ D13 Foam showers

⚂ F7 Ax'Tularian blood worm chamber

⚃ F40 Admiral Xyvqups quarters

⚄ E2 Engineering bunks

⚅ E15 Arboretum

WHITE HOLE

38

## 4 SYS-WORKS

⚀ Dimly-lit corridor on G-deck

⚁ West Pylon

⚂ H1 Quantum Core

⚃ Drive Conduit #2

⚄ G10 Waste Compactor

⚅ Televator shaft

## 5 FLIGHT DECK

⚀ J9 Escape Pod wreckage

⚁ J1 Forward repair bay

⚂ J23 Parts and supplies locker

⚃ J20 Ordinance storage area

⚄ J21 Flight holo-training creche

⚅ J30 Flight track and aft vehicle airlock

## 6 HOLDING CELLS

⚀ K19 Lavatory, torn apart by xenomorph

⚁ K18 Ambassador Qlipat's cell

⚂ K1 Security area

⚃ K12 Torture room

⚄ K6 Solitary confinement

⚅ K2 Sense-dep chamber

# ...TOO NEAR A WHITE HOLE

# OBJECTS...

## 1 WEAPONS

⚀ Gluon pistol

⚁ Phaser blade

⚂ Voice projectile harness

⚃ Monofilament nunchaku

⚄ Kruk'Chel ceremonial blade

⚅ Stasis gun (*do not fire the stasis gun*)

## 2 SENSORS

⚀ Sentience Locator Beam

⚁ Gently modified Radiation Warning Badge

⚂ Unreliable Quantum Flux Sensor

⚃ Biomedical analyzer

⚄ Vacuum Locator Device

⚅ Probability Calculation Engine

## 3 STEALTH

⚀ Personal Cloaking Device with a power problem

⚁ Sound Emission Minimizer

⚂ Surveillance drone

⚃ Holographic Image Manipulator

⚄ Sensor Dampener

⚅ Dark Field Emitter

## 4 ATTIRE

⚀ Damaged enviro-suit

⚁ Admiral Xyvqup's dress uniform

⚂ Kruk'Chel battle armor

⚃ Scavenger's rags, covered in someone's blood

⚄ Skiff pilot's helmet

⚅ Mask of the Prophet

## 5 EVIDENCE

⚀ "Theoretical" Thant-Weck quason particle

⚁ Cloned fetus

⚂ Laser-whip they used

⚃ Xenomorph-chewed corpse

⚄ Hologram recording of eyewitness testimony

⚅ Radiological anomaly scans

## 6 TALISMANS

⚀ Star map to Daluan Citadel

⚁ Quantum flux inducer *(do not activate a quantum flux inducer)*

⚂ Psychic photo of her smile

⚃ Metal cylinder containing a scalp

⚄ Crate of Ax'Tularian "wine"

⚅ Blade of the Prophet

# ...TOO NEAR A WHITE HOLE

# OPTIONAL RULE

## INEVITABLE COLLAPSE

This playset takes place aboard a space station that's slowly being torn apart by waves of quantum force from a dimensional anomaly. The characters are incompetent engineers, addicted medical officers, smugglers, pirates, prisoners, merchants, janitors, and religious fanatics—and they all want off this thing before it blows. Hilarity will doubtless ensue. Adding stunt dice to the mix can ramp up the chaos even more.

WHITE HOLE

## COUNTDOWN TO OBLIVION

Put four stunt dice into the mix, two positive outcome and two negative outcome (the rules for using stunt dice are on page 81 of *The Fiasco Companion*).

Any time a stunt die is chosen, a chunk of Star Station Sigma is ripped off and sucked into the white hole. An occupied chunk? An important chunk? Entirely up to you. Look at the locations list for suggestions of places that are now destroyed.

When the last stunt die is chosen, the last piece of the actual station vanishes into the featureless anomaly forever. Since this event is heavily telegraphed, hopefully some *alternative* has been engineered in the interim. If not, perhaps your *Fiasco* ends early—or perhaps it continues on the other side of the white hole!

# HOLLYWOOD WIVES

## THE GOOD LIFE

Palm tree-lined streets. Glittering beaches, movie star neighbors—Beverly Hills, California.

You all lead lives of fabulous luxury and wealth. Armani handbags, Louboutin shoes, jewelry by Neil Lane, personal chefs, the best bodies money can buy—you have it all. You're living the southern California dream. Your days are spent shopping on Rodeo Drive and your nights revolve around dining with your girlfriends at the trendy hot spot du jour.

Either that, or you clean up the mess those people leave behind.

Regardless, the glamorous life isn't all it's cracked up to be. The mansion's almost in foreclosure, your financial advisors are running a Ponzi scheme, and the your philandering husband is banging the nanny. You *can't* lose it all now. If only there was some way to make all your problems disappear... forever.

## MOVIE NIGHT

*The Real Housewives of Beverly Hills* (TV), *Desperate Housewives* (TV), *Get Shorty, Intolerable Cruelty, Thirteen Women, Down and Out in Beverly Hills*

## CREDITS

Written by Jobe Bittman

Cover art by Jason Morningstar

Edited by Steve Segedy

*Hollywood Wives* was Playset of the Month for April 2012.

# HOLLYWOOD WIVES

A FIASCO PLAYSET
BY JOBE BITTMAN

# RELATIONSHIPS...

## 1 FRIENDS

⚀ Long-time neighbors

⚁ Sorority sisters

⚂ Frenemies

⚃ Of Carmella Holdenkampf

⚄ "Our girls are in the same grade at The Marlborough School"

⚅ BFFs

## 2 FAMILY

⚀ Sickeningly sweet couple

⚁ Step-parent and red-headed step-child

⚂ Mom's new boyfriend and custodial child

⚃ "Are you two twins?"

⚄ Acrimoniously divorced, constantly at each other's throats

⚅ My two moms

## 3 CRIME

⚀ Mobsters

⚁ Keepers of a dark secret

⚂ Killer and would-be victim

⚃ Securities fraudster and undercover SEC agent

⚄ Con artist and mark

⚅ Crooked accountant and client

## 4 HIGH SOCIETY

⚀ Junior League associates

⚁ Members of the same country club

⚂ "Save the American Rainforest" co-chairpersons

⚃ Film industry enthusiasts

⚄ Eventual heirs to the Holdenkampf fortune

⚅ Parent and nanny

## 5 ROMANCE

⚀ Sugar daddy and sweetheart

⚁ Secret lovers, one wants to go public

⚂ Gay lovers

⚃ Holds a secret crush

⚄ Open marriage

⚅ Dominant and submissive

## 6 WORK

⚀ A pair of one-credit IMDB pages

⚁ Employer and personal assistant

⚂ Plastic surgeon and patient

⚃ Celebrity and paparazzi

⚄ Life coach and work in progress

⚅ Personal trainer and trainee

# ...IN SWANKY LOS ANGELES

# NEEDS...

## 1  TO GET BACK YOUR GROOVE

⚀ ...by a personal actualization regimen involving kale

⚁ ...by killing your enemy's favorite pet

⚂ ...by moving a surprising amount of cocaine

⚃ ...by maxing out all of that lousy cheater's credit cards

⚄ ...by getting $250,000 in "work" done

⚅ ...by getting freaky with the pool boy

## 2 TO GET FAMOUS

⚀ ...by launching a music career

⚁ ...by getting people to think you're already famous

⚂ ...by launching your kid's modeling career

⚃ ...by marrying someone famous

⚄ ...by doing something outrageous on a reality show

⚅ ...by "leaking" naked photos/videos

## 3 TO GET RICH

⚀ ...collecting on a hefty life insurance policy

⚁ ...by kidnapping someone or some thing

⚂ ...dragging a dying fiancé to the altar

⚃ ...launching a new and completely untested product

⚄ ...bilking your investors

⚅ ...selling cut-rate time shares in a down market

WIVES

48

## 4 TO UTTERLY RUIN

⚀ …a former spouse

⚁ …anyone who gets in your way

⚂ …Carmella Holdenkampf

⚃ …an emotionally distant parent

⚄ …someone who saw too much

⚅ …a family name

## 5 TO COVER UP

⚀ …the name of the real baby daddy

⚁ …that your family's not really dead. They live in a trailer in the Ozarks.

⚂ …what happened that night in Room 13

⚃ …the fact that you are broke

⚄ …the whereabouts of your daughter's missing prescriptions

⚅ …your immodest child

## 6 TO ESCAPE

⚀ …crushing debt

⚁ …an unhappy marriage

⚂ …a federal indictment

⚃ …an air-tight contract

⚄ …sheer and utter boredom

⚅ …a stalker

# …IN SWANKY LOS ANGELES

# LOCATIONS...

## 1  SHOPPING

⚀ Barney's on Wilshire Boulevard

⚁ Shopping for jewelry at Neil Lane

⚂ Choza de Pollo on West Pico

⚃ Whole Foods

⚄ Makeup counter at Neiman Marcus

⚅ Golf pro shop

## 2 PARTY

⚀ Black-tie benefit

⚁ Art opening for a fake artist

⚂ Three Nicaraguans in a van with no wheels

⚃ Celebrity charity auction

⚄ Bachelorette party

⚅ A new hot West Hollywood night club

## 3 LEISURE

⚀ A mansion's sauna room

⚁ Drinking margaritas by the pool

⚂ The Korean Bell and Friendship pavilion in San Pedro

⚃ Yoga class

⚄ Dining at a five-star restaurant

⚅ Resort gift shop

## 4 DOCTORS AND MEDS

⚀ Marijuana dispensary

⚁ Psychologist's office

⚂ Cedars-Sinai Medical Center

⚃ "Pharmacy"

⚄ Plastic surgery consultation

⚅ Veterinary plastic surgery consultation

## 5 TRAVEL

⚀ Cruising on Mulholland Drive

⚁ Yacht dinner

⚂ Catalina Island for the weekend

⚃ Stuck in traffic on the 405

⚄ Waiting for a flight at LAX

⚅ St. Regis Hotel, Dana Point

## 6 AROUND TOWN

⚀ Capitol Records Building

⚁ Vietnamese nail salon

⚂ Betting on horses at Santa Anita

⚃ Botox party

⚄ Bunco night

⚅ The green room in Studio 11, NBC Studios Burbank

# ...IN SWANKY LOS ANGELES

# OBJECTS...

## 1 SALACIOUS

⚀ Embarrassingly awkward sex tape

⚁ Monogrammed thong

⚂ Sticky riding crop

⚃ Computer with something disturbing in the web browser cache

⚄ Incriminating sexts

⚅ Love letters with something wrong with them

## 2 TRANSPORTATION

⚀ Stretch limousine

⚁ Bright yellow Hummer

⚂ Black town car with bullet-proof windows

⚃ Yacht

⚄ Gold Piper Comanche, tail number NC2799

⚅ Felt pro-level track bike, never ridden

## 3 WEAPONS

⚀ Fireplace poker

⚁ Box of rat poison

⚂ Mercedes-Benz SLR McLaren

⚃ 9 inch stiletto heel

⚄ Rigged tanning bed

⚅ Cocaine cut with fiberglass

WIVES

## 4 MORE WEAPONS

- ⚀ Tainted Beluga caviar
- ⚁ Custom-made Perazzi shotgun
- ⚂ Super-sized bottle of bleach
- ⚃ Credit Suisse 400 troy ounce gold bullion bar
- ⚄ Bejeweled dog leash
- ⚅ Dirty Botox needle

## 5 INFORMATION

- ⚀ Paternity test results
- ⚁ Security alarm codes
- ⚂ Post-it note with several passwords
- ⚃ Pre-nuptial agreement, possibly doctored
- ⚄ Whistleblower ready to turn state's evidence
- ⚅ Map to a grave in Forest Lawn

## 6 VALUABLE OR SENTIMENTAL

- ⚀ Tattered photo of the young Holdenkampfs
- ⚁ Safety deposit box key
- ⚂ Pampered Bichon Frise puppy named "Mr. Showbiz"
- ⚃ Briefcase filled with untraceable bank notes
- ⚄ Ten kilos of "Columbian Marching Powder"
- ⚅ Picasso painting

# ...IN SWANKY LOS ANGELES

# SALEM 1692

## BEING AN ACCOUNT OF THE TRYALS OF SEVERAL WITCHES, LATELY EXECUTED IN NEW-ENGLAND

After the New Year dawned on 1692, strange afflictions have beset many of the young girls in Salem. Thought to be the precocious nonsense of children, they now suffer episodes of violence and terrifying abuse at the hands of unseen forces. Their forbidden games have brought this onslaught, and they have learned them at the hands of their very neighbors and servants.

Inevitable accusations have now followed. As young as five to as old as eighty, no resident of Salem Village or the surrounding townships, good Christians or no, old or young, are safe from the witch hunt.

1692 will be a year of misery and death for all of Salem Village.

Truly, spells and stories are not simple children's games.

## MOVIE NIGHT

*The Crucible, The Village, Luther, Day of Wrath*

## CREDITS

Written by Lillian Cohen-Moore and Logan Bonner

Cover art by Jason Morningstar

Edited by Steve Segedy

*Salem 1692* was Playset of the Month, May 2012.

# Salem
## 1692

# RELATIONSHIPS...

## 1  FAMILY

⚀ Siblings

⚁ Aunt/uncle and niece/nephew

⚂ Married into same family

⚃ Cousins

⚄ Colonist and relative from England

⚅ Parent and child

## 2  IN THE COURT

⚀ Grand jurors

⚁ Defender and accused

⚂ Sheriff and delinquent

⚃ Accuser and accused

⚄ Cellmates

⚅ Chief Justice and prosecutor

## 3  FAITH

⚀ Minister and parishioner

⚁ Fake witch and "real" witch

⚂ Believer and skeptic

⚃ Witch hunters

⚄ Deacons

⚅ Secret Catholic and close friend

# 4 WEDLOCK AND SIN

⚀ Goodman and goodwife

⚁ Repressed lust

⚂ Unrequited affection

⚃ Adulterers

⚄ Parents of illegitimate child

⚅ Widows/widowers

# 5 SOCIETY

⚀ Landowners

⚁ Teacher and student

⚂ Master and slave

⚃ Doctor and patient

⚄ Fallen women

⚅ Members of the feuding Putnam and Porter families

# 6 HISTORY

⚀ Former minister of Salem and his last tie to the town

⚁ Current and former owners of an estate

⚂ Killer and witness

⚃ Experimented with witchcraft as children

⚄ Converts to the Puritan faith

⚅ Grew up together in England

# ...IN COLONIAL SALEM

# NEEDS...

## 1 TO CLEAR YOUR NAME

⚀ ...by proving you're not a witch

⚁ ...and tarnish someone else's

⚂ ...using blackmail

⚃ ...no matter the price

⚄ ...by betraying your own blood

⚅ ...in front of the grand jury

## 2 TO BE A GOOD CHRISTIAN

⚀ ...by rooting out witchcraft

⚁ ...by punishing displays of pride

⚂ ...by making an example

⚃ ...by beating the Devil out of someone

⚄ ...by steadfastly resisting this temptation

⚅ ...by converting the heathens

## 3 TO BE A GOOD STEWARD

⚀ ...by passing on your earthly possessions to your children

⚁ ...by arranging a proper marriage

⚂ ...by upholding tradition

⚃ ...by preserving Salem Village

⚄ ...by protecting the weak

⚅ ...by serving authority

SALEM

## 4 TO GET THE TRUTH

⚀ …no matter how much pain you cause

⚁ …from a loved one

⚂ …even if it kills them

⚃ …by exposing your own secrets

⚄ …to preserve another's honor

⚅ …about a rival

## 5 TO RAISE YOUR STATION

⚀ …by stealing another's property

⚁ …above a friend's

⚂ …by bearing false witness

⚃ …to benefit your family

⚄ …by destroying another's reputation

⚅ …by marrying for money

## 6 TO SUCCUMB TO THE DEVIL

⚀ …by corrupting the youth

⚁ …by practicing witchcraft

⚂ …by giving in to lust

⚃ …by perverting Church doctrine

⚄ …by aiding heretics

⚅ …by betraying loved ones

# …IN COLONIAL SALEM

# LOCATIONS...

## 1 IN SALEM TOWN

⚀ Meeting house

⚁ Court house

⚂ Charter Street cemetery

⚃ Town common

⚄ Prison

⚅ Town Bridge

## 2 ELSEWHERE IN SALEM TOWN

⚀ Gedney's "Ship Tavern"

⚁ Ingersoll's ordinary, a place for food and lodging

⚂ Training field

⚃ Gallows Hill

⚄ Reverend's parsonage

⚅ Old meeting house

## 3 OUTSKIRTS

⚀ Witch Hill

⚁ The "Seven Men's Bounds" tree

⚂ The ferry

⚃ Jeggle's Island

⚄ Orchard Farm

⚅ The docks

## 4 FORBIDDEN PLACES

⚀ Slave's quarters

⚁ The woods

⚂ Sealed well

⚃ Barn loft where that boy died

⚄ A locked shed

⚅ Deserted Indian camp

## 5 PLACES OF TOIL

⚀ Stables

⚁ Farm with dead crops

⚂ Fishing boat

⚃ Iron works in Andover

⚄ Dodge's Grist Mill

⚅ Sailing vessel, leaving soon

## 6 THE WORLD BEYOND

⚀ Boston

⚁ Ipswich

⚂ On the ship from England

⚃ London

⚄ Plymouth Colony

⚅ New Amsterdam

# ...IN COLONIAL SALEM

# OBJECTS...

## 1 BLASPHEMOUS ARTICLES

⚀ "Voodoo" poppet

⚁ Witch's ointment

⚂ Tattered grimoire

⚃ Divining rod

⚄ Gilded Catholic crucifix

⚅ Rosary

## 2 COURT

⚀ Chief Justice's seal

⚁ Witch cake

⚂ A board and 2 tons of heavy stones

⚃ Testimony of the afflicted

⚄ Court clerk's tools

⚅ Heavy manacles

## 3 BAWDY ARTICLES

⚀ Steamy letters

⚁ Canteen of rum

⚂ Women's underclothes

⚃ Samuel Pepys' copy of the idle roguish book, *L'escholle de filles*

⚄ Silk imitation of a lady's "marigold"

⚅ Wooden dildo

## 4 SHITTE WITH SECRETS

⚀ Lectern with a hidden compartment

⚁ Marionette fashioned to appear as an apparition

⚂ Powdered wig with bloodstains inside

⚃ Hidden love poem

⚄ Buried box

⚅ Diary page admitting a child's father was an Indian

## 5 SYMBOLS OF STATUS

⚀ Deed to a large estate

⚁ Fine wool cloak

⚂ Personal library

⚃ Cloak clasp from the village beauty

⚄ Calfskin gloves with strange markings

⚅ Clay pipe with a peculiar odor

## 6 WEAPONS

⚀ Scythe

⚁ Musket

⚂ Hangman's noose

⚃ Fire iron

⚄ Axe

⚅ Sergeant's halberd

# ...IN COLONIAL SALEM

# HOME INVASION

## "WE LOVE POPPLETON TERRACE"

It's a nice middle class neighborhood with a nice mix of professional families and a nice, powerful homeowners association. Good people who get involved and know their neighbors. People who aren't afraid to tell you that the shade of blue you are painting your house is not *exactly* allowed by the association covenant.

But lately things have been unsettled around Poppleton Terrace— property values are falling, crime is rising, long-time residents have been less than receptive to the suggestions of the standards committee, and now new people are moving in.

People who are not like us. *At all.*

## MOVIE NIGHT

*Invasion of the Body Snatchers, The Burbs, Neighbors, Weeds* (TV), *The Invaders* (TV), *Donnie Darko, American Beauty, The Twilight Zone* (TV; see episodes *The Shelter, The Monsters are Due on Maple Street*)

## FURTHER FIASCOS

*Home Invasion* shares a number of locations with other playsets, making it a lovely candidate for multi-session play. *Tales from Suburbia,* in the *Fiasco* book, is one. Sharp-eyed playset enthusiasts will note others.

## CREDITS

Written by Jason Morningstar

Cover art by Jason Morningstar

Edited by Steve Segedy

*Home Invasion* was Playset of the Month for June 2012.

INVASION

# HOME
# INVASION

# RELATIONSHIPS...

## 1 HOMEOWNERS ASSOCIATION

⚀ President and Vice President

⚁ Treasurer and thief

⚂ Co-authors of the revised garbage policy

⚃ Standards committee chair and the neighbor with no standards

⚄ "We're honestly trying to work this out like two adults"

⚅ Secretary and former Secretary

## 2 SHARING

⚀ ...a deep friendship

⚁ ...a heavy burden

⚂ ...a sexually-transmitted disease

⚃ ...forbidden fruit

⚄ ...gossip over the fence

⚅ ...mutual suspicions

## 3 THE PLAN

⚀ Leader and loyal right hand

⚁ Recruiter and likely prospect

⚂ Leader and minion

⚃ Minion and accidental observer

⚄ Outsiders who want in

⚅ Minions who want out

INVASION

66

## 4 BUSINESS

⚀ Home business partners

⚁ Professional rivals

⚂ Service worker and customer

⚃ Secretly unemployed

⚄ Professional and client

⚅ Co-workers

## 5 NEIGHBORS

⚀ …that are basically strangers

⚁ …at war

⚂ …with a mutual problem

⚃ …and friends!

⚄ …but not for long

⚅ …one private, the other nosy

## 6 FAMILY

⚀ Caregiver and invalid

⚁ Parent and child

⚂ "When you are friends with Chris Nasser, you are family!"

⚃ Golden child and black sheep

⚄ "Our therapist suggested this arrangement"

⚅ Husband and husband

# ...IN POPPLETON TERRACE

# NEEDS...

## 1 TO GET INTO

⚀ ...Chris Nasser's bed

⚁ ...whatever *those* people are into

⚂ ...the Homeowners Association leadership

⚃ ...the house that seems sort of abandoned

⚄ ...somebody else's business

⚅ ...the library, to figure out what you saw

## 2 TO GET OUT

⚀ ...of Chris Nasser's bed

⚁ ...of an irritating commitment to a neighbor

⚂ ...your grill and have the whole neighborhood over

⚃ ...of the lawn and garden committee

⚄ ...your gun again

⚅ ...with the Homeowners Association lockbox

## 3 TO GET FREE

⚀ ...from an unpleasant debt

⚁ ...from the homeowners association's rules

⚂ ...from the memory of something you should not have seen

⚃ ...beer

⚄ ...advice from a licensed professional

⚅ ...of a relationship turned sour

INVASION

## 4 TO GET THE PLAN IN MOTION

⚀ ...by aggressively blending in

⚁ ...by acquiring a final recruit

⚂ ...by subverting the Homeowners Association

⚃ ...by replacing the leader

⚄ ...by completing final assembly

⚅ ...by burying the evidence

## 5 TO GET OVER

⚀ ...the accident

⚁ ...100 signatures on your petition to the Homeowners Association

⚂ ...seeing something you should never have seen

⚃ ...the embarrassment of living next to a pig sty

⚄ ...being left out, betrayed and abandoned

⚅ ...nameless fear that may soon have a name

## 6 TO GET EVEN

⚀ ...with *those* people

⚁ ...*more* support for the revised garbage policy

⚂ ...by spreading rumors

⚃ ...hedges, even if you have to trim them yourself

⚄ ...with the whole Nasser family

⚅ ...by blowing the lid off this thing


# ...IN POPPLETON TERRACE

# LOCATIONS...

## 1 CLOSE QUARTERS

⚀ Secret room, drywalled in

⚁ Shed packed with cardboard boxes

⚂ A child's bedroom, untouched for twenty three years

⚃ Storm drain at the intersection of Breezeway and Piccolo

⚄ Toilet tank in the guest bathroom under the stairs

⚅ In a packing crate, buried in the yard

## 2 THE OLD END

⚀ Cul-de-sac at the end of Avanti Way

⚁ Two identically-painted houses on Piccolo Lane

⚂ Poppleton Terrace community center and meeting room

⚃ Out-of-place mansion on Vecchio Drive

⚄ Where the fire was

⚅ The House Where People Always Come And Go

## 3 THE NEW END

⚀ Breezeway Avenue house with tin-foiled windows

⚁ Yard with something written on it in weed killer

⚂ Freedom Place, Street of the Year

⚃ The House With Too Many Animals

⚄ Corner of Freedom and Piccolo, where neighbors meet

⚅ Chris Nasser's Certified Wildlife Habitat garden

## 4 WALKABLE

- ⚀ Drainage canal behind Poppleton Terrace
- ⚁ The gazebo in Poppleton Park
- ⚂ Bike path beneath the power-lines
- ⚃ Poppleton Terrace III, a model home and 56 empty lots
- ⚄ Circular clearing in the woods where nothing grows
- ⚅ Roadside memorial on State Road 217

## 5 DRIVABLE

- ⚀ Law Offices of Cockburn and Lilley, LLC
- ⚁ Men's bathroom at Poppleton Mall
- ⚂ Law Enforcement Regional Intelligence Fusion Center
- ⚃ The Well Dressed Lady
- ⚄ Chicken Hut #6310, over in Redbud Court
- ⚅ Michelle's Tavern

## 6 BEHIND CLOSED DOORS

- ⚀ Tricked-out basement home theater
- ⚁ Garage converted into a long-term nursing care facility
- ⚂ Long-occupied house without a stick of furniture in it
- ⚃ Attic full of electronic equipment
- ⚄ The best kitchen in Poppleton Terrace
- ⚅ Living room, with a telescope looking across the street

# ...IN POPPLETON TERRACE

# OBJECTS...

## 1 NEIGHBORHOOD WATCH

⚀ Sweaty baseball cap with something tucked in the brim

⚁ Aegis brand Lineman's telephone handset

⚂ Municipal garbage truck

⚃ Dave Weatherford

⚄ Annotated copy of Major Donald Keyhoe's *Flying Saucers Are Real*

⚅ A wide open wireless router

## 2 PLAN RELATED

⚀ Calcination chamber, fully prepared

⚁ Inert Wave Shaper

⚂ Outline of Plan written in *Frühneuhochdeutsch*, Early New High German

⚃ Object 7721

⚄ Sorcha-1 and Sorcha-2

⚅ Velvet drapes, with inky wrongness beyond

## 3 HOME IMPROVEMENT

⚀ Uninstalled hot tub

⚁ Precisely manicured but vaguely offensive topiary

⚂ Stihl 10-foot pole pruner chainsaw

⚃ Home theater components still in boxes

⚄ Shrink-wrapped block containing one million dollars

⚅ DeWalt cordless nail gun

## 4 HOME DEGRADATION

- Remains of Ford Probe, on blocks, in front yard
- One liter of Tetrabutylammonium Hydroxide/methanol solution, packed in nitrogen
- Framed portrait of Adolph Hitler
- Corpse of a relative
- Cracked foundation filled with termites
- Wagner power sprayer and buckets of Chinese Red exterior paint

## 5 DISTANT AND PROFESSIONAL

- Federal wiretap and search warrant
- Unmailed letter to the Homeowners Association
- Green Touch Landscaping truck
- Foreclosure notice
- Surveyor's stakes on the wrong side of a property line
- Discrete weatherproof case attached to something with magnets

## 6 UP CLOSE AND PERSONAL

- Disturbing Japanese import
- Shotgun with home-made silencer taped to the barrel
- Dental appliance, partially melted
- Lock-defeating bump key
- 100 hours of grainy digital surveillance data
- Love note written on the back of a Green Touch Landscaping bill

# ...IN POPPLETON TERRACE

# FLIGHT 1180

## UP IN THE AIR

Baggage. Even if you think you checked it all in the terminal, you're bringing some on board with you. Baggage. Everyone's got some and in the confines of an aircraft it surrounds us and mingles together. Is this your bag or mine? Is there a better metaphorical juxtaposition in air travel than "baggage carousel," where your personal baggage gets to ride the horsies?

## STRUCTURE AND FLASHBACKS

The titular flight in this playset is meant to hold the story together, but it probably shouldn't be the whole story. While every player's character should be on 1180, to maximize the mayhem, note how coincidental that might make things—the frequent flyer is also a smuggler and his ex is on the flight with him? This is good. This is a messed-up flight. Embrace the cockamamie circumstances that put all these people on the same flight. Flights are bottlenecks.

Play out flashbacks, if you want, to LA or the Pacific islands or office towers that lead up to the flight. Play out flashbacks set during the week, the month, the decade before the flight. The first Act is a great time for this. Here's an unofficial rule to observe: to play a flashback scene, first describe what you're character's physically doing on the plane—fiddling with a watch, bugging his seat-mate, pretending to read, etc. Use dialogue if you want. It helps set up context and contrast for your flashback scene.

Be careful with flashforwards, here. If you jump ahead to *after* the flight, you let some of the tension out. Think about this: how are the people who get off the plane different from when they got on?

People are usually pretty boring on planes but this game's called *Fiasco*, so try this: make at least one Tilt element take place on the plane. That way some of Act Two's juices spill over to the flight itself.

## MOVIE NIGHT

*Airplane!, Passenger 57, Executive Decision, Ekipazh, Lost* (TV)

## CREDITS

Written by Will Hindmarch; Edited by Steve Segedy; Cover by Jason Morningstar

*Flight 1180* was Playset of the Month for July 2012.

# RELATIONSHIPS...

## 1 FAMILY

⚀ Siblings, headed home for the funeral

⚁ Cousins, estranged since the spat in school

⚂ Parent and child, withholding their love

⚃ Siblings, faking affection

⚄ Grandparent and child, straining across a gulf of years

⚅ Parent and child, reunited after months

## 2 WORK

⚀ Peers feigning camaraderie

⚁ Newly promoted boss and passed-over colleague

⚂ Irresponsible executive and responsible assistant

⚃ Responsible executive and fuck-up assistant

⚄ Comrades returning from a disastrous meeting

⚅ Rival conventioneers

## 3 COINCIDENCE

⚀ A minor or local celebrity and an eager fan

⚁ Met at the airport bar prior to the flight

⚂ Old high-school enemies reunited on the flight

⚃ The sick passenger and the doctor on board by chance

⚄ The nosy middle-seater and the flight-fearing passenger

⚅ Friends of friends oddly seated next to each other

## 4 ROMANCE

⚀ Newlyweds, coming back from a disastrous honeymoon

⚁ A devoted couple, strained to breaking by airport stress

⚂ Broke up on vacation, stuck flying back together

⚃ Just met, and made out, in the airport

⚄ Spouses trying for a second honeymoon

⚅ The cheater and the lover flying to a weekend tryst

## 5 AGENTS OF THE SKY

⚀ The smitten passenger and the oblivious flight attendant

⚁ The brand-new flight attendant and the old pro

⚂ The frequent flyer and a familiar flight attendant

⚃ The furious passenger and the indignant flight attendant

⚄ The ill flight attendant and someone who thinks he's faking

⚅ The take-charge passenger and the take-charge flight attendant

## 6 CRIME OR, WELL, "CRIME"

⚀ An ex-con and an ex-cop, seated together by chance

⚁ A con artist and a mark

⚂ Two penny-ante "fugitives" from something other than justice

⚃ First-time smugglers

⚄ Retired rival B&E experts headed toward new lives

⚅ A retired bounty-hunter and a current bond-jumper

# ...ABOARD FLIGHT 1180

# NEEDS...

## 1 TO GET AWAY

⚀ ...from the evidence left behind

⚁ ...from that bitch before it's too late

⚂ ...with the goods

⚃ ...from the bastard who bought your ticket

⚄ ...from the passenger next to you

⚅ ...with adultery

## 2 TO GET RICH

⚀ ...like in the deal

⚁ ...by inheriting more than your share

⚂ ...by selling what's inside your suitcase

⚃ ...without the others finding out

⚄ ...using inside information you don't have yet

⚅ ...off the insurance money

## 3 TO GET BACK

⚀ ...in time for the funeral

⚁ ...your freedom

⚂ ...to the way things were before this trip

⚃ ...your passport

⚄ ...without anyone finding out you were gone

⚅ ...your reputation as a badass

## 4  TO GET LAID

⚀ …before you return to your ordinary life

⚁ …in the freaking sky!

⚂ …to prove you can do better than last time

⚃ …and not regret it

⚄ …without getting caught

⚅ …to know that you still can

## 5  TO GET RESPECT

⚀ …that's long overdue, that you fucking earned

⚁ …that you lost on this trip

⚂ …from that asshole who got what's yours

⚃ …from your dead father

⚄ …from the press

⚅ …from these fucking passengers

## 6  TO GET THE TRUTH

⚀ …about your inheritance

⚁ …about why they left

⚂ …about who sold you out

⚃ …about why it ended so badly

⚄ …about why you were overlooked

⚅ …and then tell the whole world about it

# …ABOARD FLIGHT 1180

# LOCATIONS...

## 1 IN THE AIR

⚀ The emergency exit row

⚁ Down in the hold

⚂ The suffocating airplane bathroom

⚃ Row 3, in the first-class cabin

⚄ Row 22, by the window

⚅ The galley, with the curtain drawn

## 2 AROUND THE AIRPORT – FLASHBACK

⚀ The crowded cab stand at the hotel

⚁ On the shuttle bus with half a dozen other poor schlubs

⚂ In the smoking lounge at the airport

⚃ In the handicapped stall of the airport bathroom

⚄ A half-assed airport franchise bar and grill

⚅ At the ticket counter, behind an irate customer

## 3 BACK HOME – FLASHBACK

⚀ In the bedroom, before this whole mess started

⚁ In the car, just after the accident

⚂ At the hospital, before you knew how bad it was

⚃ At work, when you got the assignment

⚄ In the kitchen, when you began to suspect

⚅ At the Rusty Nail, after closing, when there was still hope

## 4 WAY BACK WHEN – FLASHBACK

⚀ The bathroom in high school, before you knew better

⚁ In the burning garage, just before the worst of it

⚂ At the hospital, the day you met, you think

⚃ In the restaurant, celebrating the big day

⚄ That day in the elevator, when you lied

⚅ In the alley behind the jewelry shop

## 5 POINT OF DEPARTURE – FLASHBACK

⚀ The convention floor, with just an hour left to go

⚁ The Tasty Place Noodle House, just as they're trying to close

⚂ Club Intensity, where they dance in cages

⚃ The rooftop restaurant, which spins too fast

⚄ The hotel bathroom, morning of the flight

⚅ The convenience store at an inconvenient hour

## 6 FINAL DESTINATION

⚀ In a field of wildflowers, near the emergency slide

⚁ In the woods, where they'll never find you. Maybe.

⚂ The booking room of a New York police station

⚃ The lawyer's office, later than you should be there

⚄ In the ICU, where the machines chirp like birds

⚅ The morgue

# ...ABOARD FLIGHT 1180

# OBJECTS...

## 1 EMBARRASSING

⚀ Pornography, lots of pornography

⚁ Love letters you never sent

⚂ Your pay stub

⚃ Prescription you need to get filled

⚄ Your underwear, not where it should be

⚅ Toupee, on backwards

## 2 CONTRABAND

⚀ 4.5 oz. of foreign alcohol

⚁ Load of pirated DVDs

⚂ Leaky balloon of heroin

⚃ Just enough marijuana to secure a trafficking charge

⚄ Knife, let on the plane by accident

⚅ Small stack of fresh passports

## 3 SENTIMENTAL

⚀ Wedding band, ruined

⚁ The photo, all that's left

⚂ The ticket stub, from back when

⚃ Watch, not technically given to you

⚄ Locket with a key inside

⚅ Wedding band, thought lost

FLIGHT
1180

# 4 INFORMATIONAL

⚀ Cell phone with telling contacts in it

⚁ An iPad with your diary on it

⚂ Newspaper that says what you did, if you read it right

⚃ Digital camera with photos of you doing what you did

⚄ Receipts, which don't support your lies

⚅ Her voicemail message, which is probably a lie

# 5 VALUABLE

⚀ Diamond ring, engraved for someone else

⚁ $14,000 in small bills

⚂ Endorsed check for $22,498.00

⚃ Prototype next generation smart phone

⚄ First-edition book that's worth more than your house

⚅ Design for the next big project

# 6 SECRET

⚀ Conversation, overheard

⚁ Air marshal's Zippo lighter

⚂ The plan, all written out

⚃ A confession, meant just for one person

⚄ A promise that may yet be kept

⚅ A child, hidden away

# ...ABOARD FLIGHT 1180

# HK TPK

## INTERESTING TIMES

Hong Kong, June 1997: Over 150 years of British rule is drawing to a close, and everybody is scrambling to make their mark before the handover. The Crown Colony is a pressure-cooker of energy and uncertainty, and nobody is sure who is going to come out on top—it's the world's most exclusive night club, an hour before closing. With guns. Lots of guns.

From the triad gangsters to the cops to the big-business taipans, the players are in motion and everybody has got something in the pot. Old man Liang is packing up and heading to Canada. Helen Chu's brother works for the government, and he says the PRC is going to lock everything down. Jimmy Wong says he's going nowhere because where there's uncertainty, there's money to be made.

As the old saying goes, *when the winds of change blow, some build walls and others build windmills.*

## MOVIE NIGHT

*The Killer, Hard Boiled, A Better Tomorrow I & II, Infernal Affairs, Election, Full Contact, City On Fire, Bullet in the Head, Fulltime Killer, Triangle, Fallen Angels.*

## CREDITS

Written by Corey Reid, John Rogers, and Gareth-Michael Skarka

Cover art by Jason Morningstar

Edited by Steve Segedy

*HK TPK* was Playset of the Month for August 2012.

# RELATIONSHIPS...

## 1 CRIME

⚀ Impatient boss and talented, moody gunman

⚁ Punks out to make their name

⚂ Mortal rivals jockeying for the same big score

⚃ Cop and the untouchable criminal

⚄ "Sure I'm on the take. Good thing you've got money."

⚅ Visiting foreign "consultant" and local host

## 2 FAMILY

⚀ Siblings on opposite sides of the law

⚁ Powerful boss and nephew who gets no respect

⚂ Unknowingly related—*closely* related

⚃ Parent and child, both lying

⚄ Always in older sibling's shadow

⚅ Orphans, bound by a deadly secret

## 3 HISTORY

⚀ "Our loved ones were killed by the same people"

⚁ Debt of honor

⚂ Mentor and student

⚃ The Kai-Tak job, when some of the score went missing

⚄ Survivors of the epic shootout

⚅ "If not for you, I would have gotten away with it"

# 4 ROMANCE

⚀ Star-crossed lovers

⚁ Obsessed crush and unknowing object

⚂ Estranged but bound by fate

⚃ Contenders for the same heart

⚄ Earth-shattering sex, that one time, long ago, far away

⚅ Newlyweds, one with a secret

# 5 SIN

⚀ Adulterers, one with a dangerous spouse in play

⚁ Addict and supplier

⚂ The sex is good, but money changes hands every time

⚃ Blackmailer and mark

⚄ Partners in addiction

⚅ Trusting boss and backstabbing lieutenant

# 6 STRANGE

⚀ Assassin and beloved target

⚁ Killer and victim who survived

⚂ Citizen and (maybe) ghost

⚃ Amnesiac and secret keeper

⚄ Could be twins, but not even related

⚅ Savant with skills and the one who knows how to trigger them

# ... BEFORE THE HANDOVER

# NEEDS...

## 1 TO GET REVENGE

[⚀] ...by framing someone your enemy loves

[⚁] ...for all those years in prison

[⚂] ...on those who forced you out

[⚃] ...by burning it all down

[⚄] ...by gently taking the reins of power

[⚅] ...for what happened to Uncle Mao

## 2 TO GET RESPECT

[⚀] ...so you can finally lead your own crew

[⚁] ...from your dead father

[⚂] ...From Brother Lao of the Hundred Circle Gang

[⚃] ...or die trying

[⚄] ...by proving you can take it

[⚅] ...by pulling the biggest score ever

## 3 TO GET THE TRUTH

[⚀] ...about that night in Two Doves Alley

[⚁] ...about why they shot you in the head

[⚂] ...about what happened to the girl in the photograph

[⚃] ...about who *knows*

[⚄] ...about how Wong got back to town before you

[⚅] ...about why they didn't shoot you in the head

## 4 TO GET SQUARED AWAY

⚀ ...in the month you have left to live

⚁ ...and prove you can be trusted again

⚂ ...because you promised her as she died that you would

⚃ ...even though you know a double-cross is coming

⚄ ...and show these heartless bastards the meaning of honor

⚅ ...because you have nothing left

## 5 TO GET OUT

⚀ ...of a dangerous gambling debt

⚁ ...of a relationship that has turned weird

⚂ ...of Hong Kong before the handover

⚃ ...before somebody finds out what you did

⚄ ...that deal with the slaughterhouse and these 500 pig carcasses

⚅ ...of this teahouse before the cops arrive

## 6 TO GET RICH

⚀ ...so you can pay for the surgery

⚁ ...so they won't shoot you in the kneecaps

⚂ ...so both of you can disappear

⚃ ...so you can make your play for power

⚄ ...and destroy that son of a bitch in the process

⚅ ...without your parents finding out how you did it

# ... BEFORE THE HANDOVER

# LOCATIONS...

## 1 OF CRIMINAL INTENT

⚀ Cunningly hidden, highly explosive drug lab

⚁ Dockside warehouse full of smuggled goods

⚂ Airport hangar, with an idling Learjet LJ-45

⚃ Slaughterhouse where problems... disappear

⚄ Bustling police station

⚅ Benny Chan's auto shop

## 2 WHERE PATHS CROSS

⚀ Hospital full of innocents

⚁ Two apartments with balconies that see each other

⚂ Art museum, currently hosting a most valuable collection

⚃ Dragon boat festival

⚄ Embassy dinner for international business

⚅ A dove-filled church

## 3 WHERE BUSINESS CAN GET DONE

⚀ Jimmy Ting's bar

⚁ Heavenly Orchid escort house

⚂ Lucky Nines casino (with live music!)

⚃ Thirtieth floor penthouse suite

⚄ At the end of the pier

⚅ Crippled Li's noodle stand, just outside the precinct house

HK TPK

## 4 WHERE VIOLENCE TENDS TO OCCUR

- ⚀ Boats in Kowloon Bay
- ⚁ Rooftop shantytowns of Tai Kok Tsui
- ⚂ Helicopter pad on a tower rooftop
- ⚃ Old Master Tsao's Teahouse
- ⚄ The Night Market
- ⚅ Bridge. Truck. Rush hour.

## 5 LANDMARKS

- ⚀ Star ferry
- ⚁ Happy Valley racecourse
- ⚂ Victoria Peak—on the tram
- ⚃ Bird Market, Kowloon
- ⚄ Giant Buddha of Po Lin Monastery
- ⚅ Man Mo Temple

## 6 ODDITIES

- ⚀ Chung King tenements
- ⚁ The Yao family shrine, high up on the hillside
- ⚂ The sets for a new martial arts epic
- ⚃ Police academy graduation
- ⚄ A crowded double-decker streetcar
- ⚅ Three Moons Temple in the old neighborhood

# ... BEFORE THE HANDOVER

# OBJECTS...

## 1 GUNS

- ⚀ Rare custom-made sniper rifle with even rarer ammo
- ⚁ .45 that's killed... everyone
- ⚂ Ancient, rusty, lucky revolver
- ⚃ Derringer on a wrist slide—one shot, make it count
- ⚄ Well-used sawed-off shotgun
- ⚅ Gym bag. Full of guns.

## 2 NOT GUNS

- ⚀ Beat-up machete
- ⚁ Bomb with a twitchy trigger
- ⚂ Twin pearl-handled butterfly knives
- ⚃ Unlimited supply of rocket-propelled grenades
- ⚄ "Not *a* hammer—*the* hammer."
- ⚅ Venom of a coral sea snake

## 3 INFORMATION

- ⚀ Mickey Zhao's left thumb, on ice
- ⚁ Security video revealing who really robbed Benny Chan
- ⚂ Coded notebook detailing numerous sins
- ⚃ Timetable of International Security Agency armored cars
- ⚄ A witnesses real name and location
- ⚅ The mole's mobile phone with all his contacts

HK TPK

# 4 VALUABLE

- ⚀ One dozen blank, genuine US passports
- ⚁ Twenty million in diamonds, surrounded by guys with guns
- ⚂ Plates for a perfect 500 Euro note
- ⚃ Mercedes in the kidnap job (victim optional)
- ⚄ Rare bird worth millions
- ⚅ Shipment of children's toys, stuffed with heroin

# 5 TRANSPORTATION

- ⚀ An ambulance, a pregnant lady, and a pissed-off doctor
- ⚁ Paraglider stowed on the roof of the Bank of China tower
- ⚂ Four hundred cop cars
- ⚃ Motorcycle, still revving
- ⚄ Two speedboats
- ⚅ Waiting limousine

# 6 SENTIMENTAL

- ⚀ Dice, the owner of which cannot be killed—or so they say
- ⚁ Napkin with a lipstick kiss and a disconnected phone number
- ⚂ Sad harmonica tune
- ⚃ One wedding dress, never used
- ⚄ Blood-stained locket, inscribed with a children's rhyme
- ⚅ Luckiest deck of playing cards in Hong Kong

# ... BEFORE THE HANDOVER

# HEROES OF PINNACLE CITY

## THE WORLD TEETERS...

...on the brink of disaster! Madmen with doomsday devices, countless alien races poised to invade, meddlesome time-travellers, inter-dimensional conquerors, vampires in government, and demons in coffee shops. The super-powered heroes of Pinnacle City are all that stands between the earth and total annihilation. Now if only they would do something about it instead of arguing with each other and hiding behind their secret identities.

Pinnacle City is the center of heroism, villainy, politics and catastrophe. Hardly a day passes without someone holding the city ransom or blowing up a large portion of it. Maybe you're a hero trying to have a normal life while keeping the world safe. Maybe you're an official trying to make those damned heroes get over their egos and petty squabbling and help, or to expose them for what they really are. Perhaps you're the villain with his finger on the button, poised to show the world what you're capable of. Or, just maybe, you're an ordinary citizen caught in the middle of it all.

## MOVIE NIGHT

*The Incredibles*, *Mystery Men*, *Megamind*, *Watchmen*, *the Avengers*, and many other more traditional superhero movies (check your local listings).

## VALIANT HEROES TAKE NOTE

It might be that you're a mundane guy with no special abilities. If so, awesome! But if your character is a hero or villain with special powers, gadgets, whatever, it's helpful to nail down what they are as you create your character. (And you can always retcon powers if you need to—Superman does it all the time!)

## CREDITS

Written by Ryan Consell, Josh Hoey, Anna Kreider, and Kit Kreider

Cover art by Anne Kreider

Edited by Steve Segedy

*Heroes of Pinnacle City* was Playset of the Month for September 2012.

# HEROES OF
# PINNACLE CITY

## A FIASCO PLAYSET BY
## RYAN CONSELL, JOSH HOEY,
## ANNA KREIDER, AND KIT KREIDER

# RELATIONSHIPS...

## 1 ALLIES!

⚀ Mentor and apprentice

⚁ "Equals" on the "team"

⚂ Forced alliance

⚃ Leader and overly ambitious second-in-command

⚄ "You have to fix everything he breaks"

⚅ ...despite hideously mismatched powers

## 2 RIVALS!

⚀ Righteous defender and arch-nemesis

⚁ Champions of incompatible forms of justice

⚂ Competing for the same prize

⚃ "There can be only one"

⚄ Quarreling siblings

⚅ Vigilante and by-the-book

## 3 SECRET IDENTITIES!

⚀ Office co-workers

⚁ Hero/villain and the reporter obsessed with true identity

⚂ Mundane best friends, masked mortal enemies

⚃ You love them, but they only love the mask

⚄ You know each other's darkest secret

⚅ They know your true identity and use it as leverage

HEROES

# 4 ROMANCE!

⚀ Lovers on opposite sides of the law

⚁ Soon to be married (this time for sure)

⚂ "I can't—my superpowers would kill you."

⚃ Mundane rivals, masked lovers

⚄ "How many times are you going to stand me up?"

⚅ You remember, they don't—time travel makes you sad

# 5 ORIGIN STORIES!

⚀ "At last! Another one like me!"

⚁ Dimensional doppelgangers, or maybe just regular old clones

⚂ Amnesiac and the only one who knows the truth

⚃ "Our paths have crossed over the centuries"

⚄ "You made me what I am today!"

⚅ Parent and unknown progeny

# 6 THE GOVERNMENT!

⚀ Scientist and experiment

⚁ President and advisor

⚂ Military leader and personal security

⚃ Heroes of warring states

⚄ Powerful Senator and focal point of her crusade

⚅ Pinnacle City's Mayor and the Lord of Crime

# ...IN PINNACLE CITY

# NEEDS...

## 1  TO CONQUER THE WORLD

⚀ ...so that you can be Emperor

⚁ ...and then destroy this miserable rock

⚂ ...and bring about eternal peace

⚃ ...and hand it over to your extraterrestrial masters

⚄ ...to show them exactly how "useless" you really are

⚅ ...to add it to your collection

## 2  TO GET LAID

⚀ ...to prove that you're still human

⚁ ...to continue your species

⚂ ...to make them jealous

⚃ ...because you have damn well earned it

⚄ ...to misdirect their well-founded suspicion

⚅ ...to shake off all the horror and angst

## 3  TO ESCAPE

⚀ ...back to your own world

⚁ ...before the League of Supervillains figures out what you did

⚂ ...and go back to being a normal person

⚃ ...from the evil forces that control your actions

⚄ ...from this life of crime

⚅ ...before your terrible mistake kills you like it killed them

HEROES

## 4 TO SAVE THE DAY

⚀ ...and atone for past failures

⚁ ...so the suffering ends with you

⚂ ...so they'll celebrate you like the hero you are

⚃ ...because this is your cross to bear

⚄ ...because this? Right here? It's all your fault

⚅ ...so they'll finally admit your genius

## 5 TO GET REVENGE

⚀ ...for trapping you in that hell dimension that one time

⚁ ...against the small minds that called you a monster

⚂ ...for hurting the people you loved

⚃ ...for taking away the only thing that ever mattered

⚄ ...for keeping you from your rightful reward all these years

⚅ ...for humiliating you in your moment of triumph

## 6 TO FIND OUT

⚀ ...where she went, and why

⚁ ...what really happened at Fairweather

⚂ ...who is under that magnificent mask

⚃ ...what it is you've forgotten

⚄ ...whether he's worthy of your love

⚅ ...who will be your new sidekick

# ...IN PINNACLE CITY

# LOCATIONS...

## 1 EXOTIC

⚀ Tsiolkovsky Crater, far side of the Moon

⚁ Summit of Mt. Everest

⚂ Experimental space station Fairweather-1

⚃ An alien world in a distant galaxy

⚄ Forgotten monastery

⚅ Geothermally-heated jungle valley in Antarctica

## 2 FAMOUS

⚀ Eiffel Tower

⚁ Pyramids of Giza

⚂ White House lawn

⚃ United Nations building, New York

⚄ US-Atlantis Memorial Peace Atoll

⚅ Sydney Opera House

## 3 BORING

⚀ High-rise apartment

⚁ Suburban home

⚂ Swanky party at Fairweather Industries

⚃ Pinnacle City Panthercats football stadium

⚄ The sewers beneath Pinnacle City

⚅ Top Grind coffee shop

## 4 HEADQUARTERS

⚀ Mid-Atlantic Ridge, 100km north of Krafla, Iceland

⚁ L5 position, Earth orbit

⚂ Family mansion in Pinnacleton

⚃ Tallest skyscraper in Pinnacle City

⚄ Remote crystalline stronghold, undisclosed location

⚅ Inside Mt. Elbert, Colorado

## 5 FOUR COLOR

⚀ "My news organization is not incredibly biased!"

⚁ "This lab may be lightly guarded, but it is well funded!"

⚂ "Escape? From this super-prison? Impossible!"

⚃ "It may be illegal and we may be obvious, but the weapons still get made."

⚄ "Some people call me criminal, but I still throw a hell of a party!"

⚅ "This abandoned theme park gives me the creeps!"

## 6 PRECARIOUSLY PERCHED

⚀ ...on the slippery edge of a high-rise rooftop

⚁ ...at the lip of an erupting volcano, again

⚂ ...on top of a speeding train, airplane, or trainplane

⚃ ...in orbit, soon to plummet to Earth!

⚄ ...on the blood-slick deck of a sinking ship

⚅ ...in the path of a tsunami

# ...IN PINNACLE CITY

# OBJECTS...

## 1 NEW TECHNOLOGY

⚀ Source of limitless, free energy

⚁ Source of superpowers

⚂ Fairweather Goliath-9, the first sentient computer

⚃ Ancient alien artifact, just unearthed

⚄ 30,000 robot civil servants, ready to be activated by the Mayor

⚅ Mind control ray with unpleasant side effects

## 2 TRANSPORT

⚀ [Cool name here] mobile

⚁ Spaceship

⚂ Time machine

⚃ Armored truck

⚄ Flying fortress

⚅ Jet pack

## 3 DEVASTATION

⚀ Falling meteor!

⚁ Nuclear bomb!

⚂ Super virus!

⚃ Self-replicating nanobots!

⚄ Andromedan brain slugs!

⚅ Giantest monster ever

HEROES

## 4 WEAPONRY

⚀ Prototype freeze ray, never tested until now

⚁ Super strength ring

⚂ Calcinator death ray

⚃ Federal court injunction

⚄ Their only weakness

⚅ The most powerful laser ever built, ever

## 5 PUZZLE PIECES

⚀ Encrypted data containing their true identity

⚁ Final component of the doomsday device

⚂ Antidote, but not enough

⚃ Bank account numbers in the Caymans

⚄ Super truth serum

⚅ Key to other-dimensional portal

## 6 OMINOUS

⚀ Mask, cape and lacy underwear

⚁ Mayor's corpse

⚂ Weaponized accordion

⚃ Statuette inscribed with ancient, evil glyphs

⚄ Sealed beaker of green, glowing sludge

⚅ Abraham Lincoln's still-living brain

# ...IN PINNACLE CITY

# BACK TO THE OLD HOUSE

## THE HOUSE HAS BEEN CALLING YOU

Its dead dust breath seeping though splintered doorways. The dark hiss of long forgotten stations. Endless nights huddled in the death shed, and tears at bedtime. The house is calling, but you don't pick up.

You've tried to forget, to make a fresh start and be somebody new, but it's all bullshit. Everything that counts for anything went down in that fucking house. Bad things happened, and you were a part of it. You left unfinished business. That's why you need to go back. To finish it. To end it all.

You would rather not go back to the old house.

But you will.

## MOVIE NIGHT

*Mulholland Drive, Sapphire and Steel, Pan's Labyrinth, The Changeling, The Haunting (original version), A Tale of Two Sisters, Let the Right One In*

## BOOK CLUB

*The October Country, Happy Like Murderers*

## PUMP UP THE VOLUME

*Winter in the Belly of a Snake, Hatful of Hollow*

## SPECIAL RULE

At the end of the Aftermath, after the dice are gone, players should describe something good that happens in the future at the site where the house once stood.

## CREDITS

Written by Sean Buckley

Cover art by Jason Morningstar

Edited by Steve Segedy

*Back to the Old House* was Playset of the Month for October 2012.

# BACK
## TO THE OLD
# HOUSE

A FIASCO PLAYSET BY SEAN BUCKLEY

# RELATIONSHIPS...

## 1 BETRAYAL

- ⚀ Benefactor and impostor
- ⚁ Protector and unprotected
- ⚂ Blackmailer and victim
- ⚃ Bully and bullied
- ⚄ Buyer and seller
- ⚅ Agent and double agent

## 2 OBLIGATION

- ⚀ Feeder and fed
- ⚁ Jailor and jailed
- ⚂ Clown and machinist
- ⚃ Master and servant
- ⚄ Butcher and meat-hook
- ⚅ Nurse and patient

## 3 FAMILY

- ⚀ Childhood accomplices
- ⚁ ...in name only
- ⚂ Parent and child
- ⚃ Auntie Beryl and Uncle Death
- ⚄ "It made us from the same old bones"
- ⚅ Rival/devoted siblings

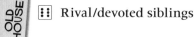

OLD HOUSE

106

## 4 IN DREAMS

- ⚀ Amnesiac and fantasist
- ⚁ Ancient child and imaginary friend
- ⚂ "We dream the same dream"
- ⚃ Hunter and hunted
- ⚄ "It landed in the desert and we took it home"
- ⚅ One heard the voices, one made the plan

## 5 LOCAL NEWS

- ⚀ Concerned neighbor and neighbor from Hell
- ⚁ Radio DJ and creepy folk musician
- ⚂ Paranormal investigator and podcaster
- ⚃ Law enforcement officer and fugitive
- ⚄ Photographer and victim
- ⚅ Washed up celebrity and notorious graffiti artist

## 6 HOUSEHOLD CHORES

- ⚀ Chef and meal
- ⚁ Plumber and saboteur
- ⚂ Architect and builder
- ⚃ Decorator and debt collector
- ⚄ Cleaner and dirt
- ⚅ Gravedigger and murderer

# ...IN THE OLD HOUSE

# NEEDS...

## 1 TO FEED

⚀ ...the family, whatever the consequences

⚁ ...lies to the hunters

⚂ ...a prisoner, or *on* a prisoner

⚃ ...something very big into something very small

⚄ ...intercepted data to an addict

⚅ ...one pet to another pet

## 2 TO BUILD

⚀ ...a trap to set us free

⚁ ...an addition to the house

⚂ ...a machine that will do our work long after we are gone

⚃ ...a bridge that might take us truly home

⚄ ...furnishings from flat-packed kits

⚅ ...an exact replica of something incredibly complicated

## 3 TO GET REVENGE

⚀ ...on the family

⚁ ...on a murderer

⚂ ...on a coward

⚃ ...on a traitor

⚄ ...on the one who forgave you

⚅ ...on the one who brought you back

OLD HOUSE

108

## 4 TO CONTROL

⚀ ...the pain from the wound and/or operation

⚁ ...dangerous emissions

⚂ ...the food supply

⚃ ...the volume

⚄ ...an overwhelming sense of guilt, grief or shame

⚅ ...the crowds that seem to be gathering

## 5 TO EXPOSE

⚀ ...the lie that holds everything together

⚁ ...your own skeletons

⚂ ...your naked flesh to the baying mob

⚃ ...a parasite

⚄ ...the truth about what they did to you

⚅ ...what's really on the menu

## 6 TO BE LOVED

⚀ ...until Tuesday

⚁ ...by the mourners

⚂ ...by the voices

⚃ ...by the family

⚄ ...by the Old Ones

⚅ ...by your victims

# ...IN THE OLD HOUSE

# LOCATIONS...

## 1 TRANSPORT

⚀ Elevator

⚁ Ghost train

⚂ The rear of the last night bus

⚃ Old burnt-out car in the woods

⚄ Clinging to the back of a demon

⚅ Tandem bicycle

## 2 CRIME SCENES

⚀ Caravan you grew up in

⚁ Behind the big iron gate at the scrapyard

⚂ Behind the bins at a service station

⚃ Room where all the killing will happen

⚄ Room where all the kissing did happen

⚅ Top floor of the Crestmoor, Upper West Side, New York City

## 3 DARKNESS

⚀ ...in a beautiful sun-lit garden

⚁ ...under the monster's bed

⚂ ...and death on the stairs

⚃ ...at a terrible performance

⚄ ...in the little box

⚅ ...in the tunnels under the house

OLD
HOUSE

110

## 4 OUTSIDE

⚀ At the crossroads

⚁ On the bridge

⚂ Immediately after the accident

⚃ At another funeral

⚄ ...the hospital incinerator

⚅ In the long, dark trenches

## 5 BETWEEN THE CRACKS

⚀ An impossible beach

⚁ In the fire of burning souls

⚂ In a rowboat with a dead hare

⚃ Inside a hologram of her bedroom

⚄ Lost in television

⚅ Trapped under the ice

## 6 HOME COMFORTS

⚀ Radio room

⚁ Cupboard under the stairs

⚂ Basement pump room

⚃ Forgotten attic *Wunderkammer*

⚄ Dark stairway to the battlefield

⚅ "Feeding paraphernalia" room

# ...IN THE OLD HOUSE

# OBJECTS...

## 1 FOOD AND DRINK

⚀ Leftovers from the feast

⚁ An unhappy meal

⚂ Sound and vision

⚄ Fresh, warm, and wriggling

⚄ In a black plastic bag in the back of the wardrobe

⚅ Soul soup

## 2 APPLIANCES

⚀ Feeding equipment

⚁ Radio that broadcasts the dreams of the dead

⚂ Humming medical pump

⚃ Walk-in freezer with multiple padlocks

⚄ Huge archaic switchboard

⚅ Camera that puts the dead people back

## 3 WORKING FROM HOME

⚀ Comfy chair

⚁ Regrettable contracts

⚂ Hidden CCTV

⚃ Surgical instruments

⚄ Instruction manual

⚅ Projector of an unusual sort

OLD
HOUSE

112

## 4 DANGEROUS

⚀ Last Will & Testament

⚁ Box of old letters

⚂ Cage

⚃ "Get better" medicine

⚄ Faulty generator

⚅ Valium harpoon

## 5 HIDDEN

⚀ Photographs that should stay hidden

⚁ Diary that should never be read

⚂ Costume that should not be worn

⚃ Partially completed to-do list

⚄ Tragic confessional letter

⚅ Doorway connecting physically unconnected places

## 6 KEEPSAKES

⚀ Chunks of meat

⚁ Scars

⚂ Murder weapon

⚃ Cattle prod with "happy smiles" scratched on its casing

⚄ Bottle of tears

⚅ Dirty skeleton in an old sports bag

# ...IN THE OLD HOUSE

# TARTAN NOIR

## NOT SO BONNIE SCOTLAND

There's been a murder. A body lies dead in a run-down apartment. There are signs of a struggle. Broken furniture litters the floor. Two of the victim's fingers have been cut off. There's a human turd on the mantelpiece. Hang on, what?

Welcome to the world of Tartan Noir: fiction with a hardboiled, cynical, violent and frequently alcoholic view of crime in modern-day Scotland. There are good guys, there are bad guys, but there definitely aren't any heroes. Tartan Noir is about world-weary anti-heroes, deeply flawed characters with a variety of vices that would not normally be becoming of someone of their narrative stature.

And while it is certainly hardboiled, there's frequently an edge of wackiness that separates Tartan Noir from its American cousin. Retired detectives running around oil rigs in their pyjamas. Christian extremists trapped in an art gallery full of pornography. And of course the aforementioned jobby on the mantelpiece. It's grim, it's grisly, but it's a hell of a lot of fun. So pour yourself a dram of single malt and prepare to indulge in a little Tartan Noir.

## A WEE BIT OF LIGHT READING...

This playset is heavily inspired by Scottish crime writers, in particular Ian Rankin and Christopher Brookmyre. Any of Rankin's *Inspector Rebus* series and Brookmyre's *Where the Bodies are Buried* and *When the Devil Drives* would be excellent fuel for your hardboiled, whisky-drinking anti-hero. For a touch of whimsical craziness, Brookmyre's *Jack Parlabane* or *Angelique de Xavia* novels will provide excellent inspiration.

## ...AND SOME THINGS TO WATCH

To give you the true Scottish feel with a Tartan Noir edge the best possible viewing would be the television series *Taggart* and the Ken Stott adaptation of *Rebus*. The movies *Shallow Grave, Trainspotting*, and *Young Adam* will also help to develop your cynical, binge drinking, Scottish streak. Finally, no Tartan Noir is complete without some miserable bastards and creative Scottish swearing. For that there is nothing better than the omnishambles of characters that make up *The Thick of It*.

## CREDITS

Written by DC Bradshaw; Edited by Steve Segedy (with thanks to Gregor Hutton); Cover art by Jason Morningstar

*Tartan Noir* was Playset of the Month for November 2012.

# TARTAN NOIR

## DC Bradshaw

# RELATIONSHIPS...

## 1 FAMILY

⚀ Siblings

⚁ Cousins

⚂ Parent and (step) child

⚃ In-laws

⚄ Curious youngster and that older relative we don't talk about

⚅ Unknowingly related

## 2 FRIENDSHIP

⚀ Work colleagues

⚁ Drinking pals

⚂ Mates since school/college

⚃ Friends with far too much sexual tension

⚄ Friends with benefits

⚅ House mates

## 3 ROMANCE

⚀ Spouses

⚁ Ex-spouses

⚂ Life-long crush

⚃ One-night standees

⚄ Lovers

⚅ Former lovers

TARTAN NOIR

## 4 CIVILIAN WORK

⚀ Pub landlord/worker and regular

⚁ Doctor and patient

⚂ Teacher and pupil

⚃ Tour guide and tourist

⚄ Office worker and boss

⚅ Escort and client

## 5 CRIME

⚀ Drug dealer and supplier

⚁ Small-time thieves/burglars

⚂ Neds with a proud set of ASBOs

⚃ Ex-convict and parole officer

⚄ Corrupt CEO/government official and employee

⚅ Crime boss and underling

## 6 INVESTIGATION

⚀ Journalist and photographer/editor/source

⚁ CID/uniformed polis officer and superior/partner/suspect

⚂ Special branch investigator and suspect

⚃ Ex-armed forces and contact

⚄ Nosey amateur and contact

⚅ Post-mortem physician and contact

# ...IN A CITY IN SCOTLAND

# NEEDS...

## 1  TAE GET PISHED

⚀ ...'cause it's the weekend

⚁ ...'cause they're gone

⚂ ...'cause it's all gone to shite

⚃ ...'cause it's all gone right for once

⚄ ...'cause it's been a while

⚅ ...'cause you can

## 2  TAE GET PAY BACK

⚀ ...on the neds who robbed you

⚁ ...on the weegie who gave you that smile

⚂ ...on the two-faced bastard/bitch who betrayed you

⚃ ...on the bawbag who fucked it up for you

⚄ ...on maw/da for what they did when you were young

⚅ ...on the polis (just 'cause)

## 3  TAE GET MINTED

⚀ ...by selling that thing you've been holding on to

⚁ ...by doing a pal a "favour"

⚂ ...by selling that story to the press

⚃ ...by robbing a bank

⚄ ...by making them deid

⚅ ...by making it look like an accident

TARTAN NOIR

118

## 4  TAE GET HAME

⚀ ...to the love of your life

⚁ ...'cause you've served your time

⚂ ...and start a new life

⚃ ...and say what you should have said a long time ago

⚄ ...before they get there first

⚅ ...'cause you have no fucking clue where you've woken up

## 5  TAE GET TAE THE BOTTOM OF

⚀ ...who killed them

⚁ ...where they're hiding

⚂ ...why they let themselves get caught

⚃ ...what happened to all that money

⚄ ...when they removed the evidence

⚅ ...how they escaped

## 6  TAE GET IT DONE

⚀ ...while they're away

⚁ ...before it's too late

⚂ ...'cause it's been put off for far too long

⚃ ...before you get caught

⚄ ...before you pish yourself

⚅ ...before the bomb explodes

# ...IN A CITY IN SCOTLAND

# LOCATIONS...

## 1 RESIDENTIAL

⚀ Tourist bed-and-breakfast

⚁ Backpacker's hostel

⚂ Comfortable three-bedroom house

⚃ University halls of residence

⚄ Death-trap flat

⚅ Sleeping bag outside an RBS

## 2 COMMUNITY

⚀ Pulpit of a local church

⚁ Overnight cells in a police station

⚂ Hospital waiting room

⚃ In the middle of the park

⚄ An RBS branch

⚅ That cafe where that person wrote that book

## 3 TRANSPORT

⚀ Car dealership

⚁ Deserted train station, late at night

⚂ Smashed-up Bus shelter

⚃ Airport

⚄ Down by the docks

⚅ On a tram, still locked in a warehouse

TARTAN NOIR

120

## 4 SHADY PLACES

- ⚀ Down by the river
- ⚁ In a pub toilet
- ⚂ Behind the sex shop
- ⚃ In the back room of a sauna
- ⚄ On the dance floor
- ⚅ In the underground car park

## 5 AULD REEKIE

- ⚀ On the Royal Mile during the Festival
- ⚁ At the top of the Scott Monument
- ⚂ On the pitch at Murrayfield Stadium
- ⚃ Under the city in Mary King's Close
- ⚄ On the steps of Fleshmarket Close
- ⚅ In the back room of the Oxford Bar

## 6 GLESCAE

- ⚀ Under a seat in the Theatre Royal
- ⚁ In the changing rooms at Ibrox
- ⚂ Vault in the Burrell Gallery
- ⚃ At the foot of the Finnieston Crane
- ⚄ Buried in the Necropolis
- ⚅ Under the Duke's cone

# ...IN A CITY IN SCOTLAND

# OBJECTS...

## 1 TOURIST TAT

⚀ A "see you, Jimmy" hat

⚁ Kilt towel

⚂ CD of "traditional" music

⚃ Miniature bottle of shite whisky

⚄ Cheap knock-off rugby shirt

⚅ Mundane object with a university logo stamped on it

## 2 FOOD AND DRINK

⚀ Haggis/fish supper with chippy sauce

⚁ Rock-hard bar of tablet

⚂ Ice-cold can of Bru

⚃ Crate of Tennent's lager

⚄ Bottle of Buckie

⚅ 18-year old single malt

## 3 PERSONAL

⚀ Wedding ring

⚁ Cross on a silver chain

⚂ The medal you won that time

⚃ Passworded laptop

⚄ Pregnancy test

⚅ Set of keys ("This key here, this key is a mystery")

TARTAN NOIR

## 4 DRUGS

⚀ Couple of joints

⚁ Plate of hash brownies

⚂ Couple of bags of powder

⚃ Two dozen ecstasy tablets

⚄ Veritable shitload of heroin

⚅ Brown-papered package ("the boss said don't open it")

## 5 WEAPONS

⚀ Replica weapon, probably historical

⚁ Bottle of rat poison

⚂ Car

⚃ Broken Buckie bottle

⚄ Illegal handgun

⚅ A ceremonial sgian-dubh, tucked in a sock

## 6 WHAT THE FUCK?

⚀ Burned Rangers/Celtic shirt

⚁ Padlocked chest of adventurous sex toys

⚂ Briefcase, bulging with £1 notes

⚃ Signed album by the Proclaimers

⚄ Human turd

⚅ Clown mask

# ...IN A CITY IN SCOTLAND

# TOURING ROCK BAND 2

## IT WAS A GOOD RUN

You were supposed to live fast and die young. At least you lived fast.

Now you are not so young. Not so famous. Not quite able to rise to the sybaritic occasion the way you did back in the crazy days. Back when you were the big deal, touring the world behind an album that could have—should have—gone platinum. You had your moment and now it has passed. The band broke up, over sex and money and a lot of stuff that seems trivial now.

You've had to tone it down a little, accept a new sort of reality that involved trashing fewer hotel rooms and paying more bills on time and getting prostate exams that are actually prostate exams.

But the dreams never died, and lately the various anemic side projects have been less and less satisfying. And as bad decisions and old bridges burned come back to haunt you, the idea of revisiting past glory seems better and better. God knows you need the cash. And you still have fans on the Internet who would kill to see the band get back together…

## MOVIE NIGHT

*Anvil: The Story of Anvil, Still Crazy, Saxondale* (TV), *Tutti Frutti* (TV), *Ladies and Gentlemen, The Fabulous Stains, Last Days Here, We Jam Econo*, the third act of any movie about rock and roll including *The Doors, Rock Star,* and many others.

## SPECIAL NOTE

Maybe you already have Relationships from a session of *Touring Rock Band*. If so, feel free to keep them in mind while defining new ones. Relationships do change over time, though, so don't be shy about retaining your characters but redefining who they are to one another. You can also call back Objects and even Locations if they are especially resonant and juicy.

## CREDITS

Written by Chris Bennett, Jobe Bittman, Logan Bonner, Per Fischer, James Gabrielsen, Stephen Granade, Jérôme Larré, Megan Pedersen, Dan Puckett, John Rogers, and Gareth-Michael Skarka

Additional writing and editing by Steve Segedy and Jason Morningstar

Cover art by Jason Morningstar

*Touring Rock Band 2* was Playset of the Month for December 2012

# TOURING ROCK BAND 2:

# WHEN THE MUSIC STOPPED

# RELATIONSHIPS...

## 1 FAMILY

⚀ "Divorced. But, you know, we're cool with that"

⚁ Twins

⚂ The couple that defied the odds

⚃ Extramarital child and parent

⚄ A lie told so long it became true

⚅ Cousins

## 2 GOOD FRIENDS

⚀ High school sweethearts

⚁ Mentor and new kid with fast hands

⚂ Play the same instrument, by some definition of instrument

⚃ Rehab buddies

⚄ "Nothing has changed for us since 1990"

⚅ Composer and lyricist

## 3 THE GRIND

⚀ Coworkers at funeral monument carving workshop

⚁ New front man and old rocker

⚂ Baristas

⚃ "We're all roadies now"

⚄ Desperate visionary and the stubborn one

⚅ Boss and boss

## 4 PARASITES

- ⚀ Old musician and number one fan
- ⚁ Plastic surgeon and devoted client
- ⚂ Record executive and "artist"
- ⚃ Shiftless dreamer and spouse with job
- ⚄ Fired agent and tour personnel
- ⚅ Rock poet and social worker

## 5 TROUBLE

- ⚀ Law enforcement officer and ex-con
- ⚁ Aspiring author and ghostwriter
- ⚂ Guru and follower
- ⚃ Drug people
- ⚄ Bitter ex-spouses
- ⚅ Newest members of *King Boots Affair*

## 6 BAD FRIENDS

- ⚀ Codependent spouses
- ⚁ Misguided business partners
- ⚂ Moneylender and serious debtor
- ⚃ Cleaned-up addict and dealer
- ⚄ The one who eventually made it big and the one who never did
- ⚅ Unknown songwriter and the one who took all the credit

# ...AFTER THE MUSIC STOPS

# NEEDS...

## 1 TO GET FUCKED

⚀ ...though your body may not cooperate

⚁ ...by Marcie Lowell

⚂ ...by the record label to get your album deal

⚃ ...because you never have been

⚄ ...by that person who never would back in the day

⚅ ...by somebody you didn't marry twice

## 2 TO GET WASTED

⚀ ...while keeping your "clean living" rep

⚁ ...in the grand manner to which you were once accustomed

⚂ ...with your high school sweetheart

⚃ ...in public, on television, while getting paid

⚄ ...for one last time

⚅ ...with a living legend

## 3 TO GET A LITTLE CASH

⚀ ...from royalties you are due

⚁ ...to fund an ironic nostalgia gig at the Beanstalk

⚂ ...by moving a little product

⚃ ...from selling your rock relics on the Internet

⚄ ...to pay for all that alimony and the lawsuits

⚅ ...by scamming free stuff from fans

## 4 TO GET REVENGE

⚀ ...on *King Boots Affair*, those upstart assholes

⚁ ...for what happened on tour all those years ago

⚂ ...on Tito Luna for stealing your money

⚃ ...on the monster who stole your spouse

⚄ ...on those who made you a living joke

⚅ ...because nobody should *ever* touch another man's falcon

## 5 TO GET RESPECT

⚀ ...by finishing the magnum opus at last

⚁ ...by recovering your pawned American Music Award

⚂ ...by finally coming out of the closet

⚃ ...by filling the arena one more time

⚄ ...by playing the humanitarian card

⚅ ...by partying harder than people half your age

## 6 TO GET BACK IN

⚀ ...shape, for reasons that are pretty obvious

⚁ ...the band

⚂ ...the game, despite someone's reluctance

⚃ ...to your kid's life

⚄ ...by letting a pop star debase your life's work

⚅ ...by scoring spots in the cast of that reality TV show

# ...AFTER THE MUSIC STOPS

# LOCATIONS...

## 1 HUMBUCKER'S MUSIC STORE

⚀ Owner's office, gold records on the wall

⚁ Crawlspace beneath the drum room

⚂ Soundproofed music lesson room

⚃ Humbucker's Famous Bargain Basement

⚄ Band and orchestra rental desk

⚅ Shelf where the accounts payable ledger is supposed to be

## 2 THE PHELPS BUILDING

⚀ Amstar Studios

⚁ Law offices of Creswell Phelps

⚂ Dr. Gerlach Moeller, Urology

⚃ The Frantic Bean coffee stand

⚄ Pacific Breeze Cosmetic Surgery and Spa

⚅ Reception desk staffed by a bored rent-a-cop

## 3 THE BEANSTALK SHOW CLUB

⚀ Manager's office, usually locked

⚁ On stage, under the lights, like old times

⚂ Trough urinal, men's bathroom

⚃ Out in the van under drifts of cheeseburger wrappers

⚄ Behind the bar, slinging drinks

⚅ Green room, grotty as ever

## 4 DOWNTOWN

⚀ R. McGhee, Dental Surgery and Prosthodontics

⚁ Merlin Park Occupy encampment

⚂ Forever Records, long since boarded up and closed

⚃ Gamehawks Falconry Supply

⚄ Dumpster behind the Chicken Hut

⚅ Namaste Books and Crystals

## 5 CRASH SPACE

⚀ Crumbling mansion built ten years ago

⚁ The old bus, which will never roll again

⚂ Upscale condo paid for by an occasionally demanding fan

⚃ Some girlfriend's duplex next to the tracks

⚄ Empty swimming pool shaped like a double-necked guitar

⚅ Little cottage on the grounds of the big mansion

## 6 11 PENTECOST ROAD

⚀ On the roof, by the UFO beacon

⚁ Brody's bedroom, where he keeps the hard stuff

⚂ Basement "party" room with the hidden camera

⚃ Front porch filled with old couches and college stoners

⚄ The living room, where the bands play

⚅ Out back, in the bonfire

# ...AFTER THE MUSIC STOPS

# OBJECTS...

## 1  SICK AS HELL

⚀ Extremely old grizzly bear

⚁ Medical chart with very bad news on it

⚂ Medical marijuana in vast quantities

⚃ Lemmy Kilmister

⚄ Daily dialysis support for long-ruined kidneys

⚅ Bronzed armadillo with something engraved on it

## 2  ROCKIN'

⚀ Extraordinarily precious guitar

⚁ Bottles of pills you cannot get anywhere any more

⚂ 15-year-old pyrotechnic charges

⚃ Long lost studio masters of the second album

⚄ Schott Perfecto leather jacket

⚅ Weathered, disintegrating Scab-Man costume

## 3  ROLLIN'

⚀ The old bus, Janis

⚁ Backpack full of rubber masks and spray paint cans

⚂ KISS lunchbox full of Viagra

⚃ Gold record

⚄ New contract waiting for a signature

⚅ Tipper Gore's private phone number

# 4 FUCKIN' AWESOME

⚀ Sun-bleached carcass of a Maserati Quattroporte III

⚁ Ronnie James Dio's wristbands

⚂ The pick. *You know the one.*

⚃ Neil Peart's copy of *The Fountainhead*, extensively underlined

⚄ Two-handed sword, slightly used

⚅ 666 black M&M candies in a jar

# 5 DUDE NO WAY

⚀ Stack of paternity test results

⚁ Ten dusty boxes of merch from the final tour

⚂ Replica of a youthful schlong done by Cynthia Plaster Caster

⚃ Dangerously-trained peregrine falcon

⚄ Deceased bandmate's skull, now an honored bong

⚅ Tito Luna's stolen horse trailer

# 6 FUCKIN' WEAK

⚀ Comp tickets to a *King Boots Affair* show at the Beanstalk

⚁ Clean work uniforms

⚂ Old stage costume that you're too fat to wear

⚃ Candidacy Filing paperwork for School Board Election

⚄ Boxes of faded, tear-stained fan letters

⚅ Pile of unopened certified mail from the IRS

# ...AFTER THE MUSIC STOPS

# WELCOME TO JET CITY

## RAIN, COFFEE, SPACE NEEDLE, ETC

It's Seattle, Washington, the northwest city with the urban heart! Perched on the edge of wilderness, gateway to Alaska, the Emerald City! Sassy and hip, the birthplace of grunge, home of great coffee! The Queen City, City of Flowers!

Try to be less excited.

Here's the deal—it's going to rain and it isn't going to stop. Dope may be legal but black tar heroin junkies litter the streets like burger wrappers. The gang wars are small and relatively polite, and some of the gangs consist of organic gardeners. It's messed up.

Someday soon Mt. Ranier is going to erupt and bury the whole grey misbegotten ensemble beneath boiling pyroclastic lava. Before that happens, we need to stop grinding it out and make this town pay. Your new two thousand dollar road bike isn't going to buy itself.

## MOVIE NIGHT

*My Own Private Idaho, Humpday, Chefs of Seattle, Ten Things I Hate About You*

## BOOK CLUB

*Another Roadside Attraction, Sons of the Profits*

## CREDITS

Written by Jason Morningstar

Cover art by Jason Morningstar

Edited by Steve Segedy

Thanks to Peter Adkison and Ben Robbins

• WELCOME TO •
# JET CITY!

A FIASCO PLAYSET BY

JASON MORNINGSTAR

BUD LITE 15 PK 11.99

# RELATIONSHIPS...

## 1  FOR REAL FRIENDS

⚀ "We've got each other's names tattooed on our arms"

⚁ Share a booth at the farmer's market

⚂ Friends of Kudzu (F.O.K.)

⚃ ...with benefits

⚄ Back from King County lockup

⚅ Alleged victim and steadfast supporter

## 2  FOR SHOW FRIENDS

⚀ Mutual beards

⚁ "Don't screw this up for me"

⚂ Belay slave and climbing wall rat

⚃ Sponsored by Rage Bikes

⚄ At church, anyway

⚅ Trained together at CIA in Baking and Pastry Arts

## 3  FAMILY

⚀ Siblings and opposites

⚁ Estranged spouses

⚂ "Apparently you are my uncle"

⚃ Ex-family

⚄ Members of a cult-like social organization

⚅ Child and wayward parent

## 4 BUSINESS

⚀ Fry cooks, occasionally

⚁ Mechanic and baker at the Brakery

⚂ "We can learn as we go"

⚃ Hot shot and nobody

⚄ Consultant and consulted upon

⚅ Front end and Mr. Fixit

## 5 PLEASURE

⚀ True love

⚁ Community gardeners

⚂ Random hookup from The Stranger personals

⚃ An arrangement of convenience

⚄ "Do we love bread too much?"

⚅ Docents at the Museum of Glass

## 6 ON THE DOWN LOW

⚀ Police officer and snitch

⚁ Bigfoot hunters

⚂ Casual drug dealers

⚃ Process server and served

⚄ Public figure and embarrassment

⚅ "You're a food reporter and I need a good review"

# ...IN JET CITY

# NEEDS...

## 1 TO GET IN

⚀ ...your parents good graces again

⚁ ...Kudzu's pants

⚂ ...the Zagat guide

⚃ ...the cashbox, just this once you will *totally* pay it back

⚄ ...line, straighten up, and do right for once

⚅ ...the Rat Alley Rollergirls

## 2 TO GET ON

⚀ ...public assistance

⚁ ...the tune-up crew at The Brakery

⚂ ...Vashon Island to settle some scores

⚃ ...KOMO's bake-off

⚄ ...top of the Space Needle

⚅ ...the Rage Bikes MTB team

## 3 TO GET OUT

⚀ ...of County supervised community service

⚁ ...of a relationship you shouldn't get out of

⚂ ...a deck of Magic cards and make some easy money

⚃ ...of a marriage gone sour

⚄ ...of a bad commercial lease

⚅ ...the perfect loaf of sourdough, fresh and hot

## 4 TO GET UP

⚀ …off your ass and look for Bigfoot

⚁ …or rather to get *it* up

⚂ …the scratch to make a serious move

⚃ …the courage to ask

⚄ …to no good, because of smash capitalism!

⚅ …a decent collection for poor Alice Tung

## 5 TO GET OFF

⚀ …the kitchen scut crew at The Brakery

⚁ …on booze and pills and booze

⚂ …together but not, you know, *touching*

⚃ …the grid and live gently upon the Earth

⚄ …in the back room, regularly

⚅ …public assistance

## 6 TO GET DOWN

⚀ …into the locked basement of the Brakery building

⚁ …and dirty on some bomber singletrack out by Fort Nisqually

⚂ …on paper what you've witnessed

⚃ …with fuckin' Kudzu

⚄ …on your knees and beg for forgiveness

⚅ …town and close the deal

# ...IN JET CITY

# LOCATIONS...

## 1 EASY

⚀ On a houseboat in Lake Union

⚁ Elliott Bay Coffee and News

⚂ Seattle Public library

⚃ Yale Theater, during a revival showing of *Pandora's Box*

⚄ Aggressively modern mansion on Lake Washington

⚅ Loft apartment overlooking the Alaskan Way viaduct

## 2 BREEZY

⚀ Hand built rowboat in Lake Washington

⚁ Seattle Arboretum

⚂ d-deck conference center on the Space Needle

⚃ Alki Beach

⚄ Kerry Park, way up on Queen Anne hill

⚅ Aboard a state ferry

## 3 SLEAZY

⚀ Washed up on the muddy banks of Gasworks Park

⚁ The Last Call Room

⚂ Guadalupe Motel, not exactly a motel

⚃ Triple Seven Nails and Massage

⚄ South Pole Cafe, open all night

⚅ Construction dumpster in Ballard

## 4 QUEASY

- ⚀ King County Youth Detention Center
- ⚁ Needle exchange
- ⚂ Pho Saigon
- ⚃ Dale's Hamburgers
- ⚄ Gridlocked on the 520 bridge
- ⚅ U District telemarketing hutch

## 5 UNEASY

- ⚀ Angel's Repair & Tow
- ⚁ Freight terminal warehouse, Harbor Island
- ⚂ Downtown parking garage
- ⚃ Silence Heart Nest organic restaurant
- ⚄ Stash house in Greenlake
- ⚅ Artisanal cheesemonger's van

## 6 CHEESY

- ⚀ Pike Place Market
- ⚁ Fort Nisqually stockade
- ⚂ Audio Lightning Lounge
- ⚃ Berrydale Speedway
- ⚄ Danger Mountain Country Store
- ⚅ Just off the tour route in the Seattle underground

# ...IN JET CITY

# OBJECTS...

## 1  BUSTED

⚀ "I got this from a drunk Yakuza"

⚁ SPD handcuffs without a key

⚂ 1992 Toyota Celica 'art car'

⚃ Pair of business ledgers, one real and one full of lies

⚄ Court documents containing nothing but bad news

⚅ Espresso machine that won't hold pressure

## 2  DUSTED

⚀ Fingerprint collection and analysis kit

⚁ "If we huff this we will see God"

⚂ Laundry basket full of muddy riding gear

⚃ Corpse, covered in flour

⚄ Cocaine in a baking powder tin

⚅ Barrel of flour additive chemical azodicarbonamide, "generally recognized as safe"

## 3  TRUSTED

⚀ Mortiz starter pistol

⚁ Empire gas powered 16-pan artisan deck oven

⚂ "This is the phone number of a guy who takes care of stuff."

⚃ Sourdough starter with a gold rush lineage

⚄ Aluminum shorty baseball bat

⚅ Keys to the Museum of Glass

# 4 ADJUSTED

⚀ Foes F275 downhill racing bike in candy orange

⚁ Cessna 206 on floats

⚂ Orthopedic pin tightening wrench

⚃ "If you sign this they give you one million dollars."

⚄ Bent piccolo in a case with a broken latch

⚅ Therapist's patient notes

# 5 ENCRUSTED

⚀ Two pound bigfoot coprolite*

⚁ Filthy bread knife

⚂ $40,000 brooch with 22 carats of white diamonds

⚃ Paving stone matted with blood and hair

⚄ "This baby needs to be changed like an hour ago"

⚅ Plastic tub full of geoduck clams

# 6 LUSTED

⚀ Original artwork for the Black Lotus Magic card

⚁ Cask of perfect hard winter wheat berries from Japan

⚂ Tattered photograph with some numbers written on the back

⚃ Hand-written recipe from Silence Heart Nest restaurant

⚄ Skid Road Coffee, a turn-key franchise opportunity

⚅ "It's a printout from dateseattle.com, just take it"

# ...IN JET CITY

\* Fossilized poop (you're welcome)